The Hooligan

The
Hooligan Nights

Being the Life and Opinions of
a Young and Impertinent Criminal
Recounted by Himself
and Set Forth by Clarence Rook

With an Introduction by Benny Green

Oxford New York
OXFORD UNIVERSITY PRESS

Oxford University Press, Walton Street, Oxford OX2 6DP

Oxford New York Toronto
Delhi Bombay Calcutta Madras Karachi
Kuala Lumpur Singapore Hong Kong Tokyo
Nairobi Dar es Salaam Cape Town
Melbourne Auckland

and associated companies in
Beirut Berlin Ibadan Nicosia

Oxford is a trade mark of Oxford University Press

Introduction © Benny Green 1979

First published 1899 by Grant Richards
First issued, with Benny Green's introduction, as an Oxford University
Press paperback 1979
Reprinted 1985

British Library Cataloguing in Publication Data
Rook Clarence
The hooligan nights.
1. Gants—England—London—History
I. Title
364.1'066'0926   HV6439.G72L/ 79-40302

ISBN 0-19-281256-4

Printed in Great Britain by
The Guernsey Press Co. Ltd.
Guernsey, Channel Islands

Contents

Introduction

Ever since Defoe and Fielding established the convention, the habitual criminal has been a useful stick with which to beat the bourgeoisie. Crusoe's deadly observation that necessity makes an honest man a knave is at any rate more worldly-wise than the stance of the sabbatarians of the Victorian age who proceeded on the assumption that a sniff of brimstone will turn a knave into a pewholder, and whose purgative draughts of restrictive legislation were dismissed by Dickens as 'saintly venom'. Defoe at least had experience on his side; it was because circumstances flung him into the stewpot of urban penury that he was able to write of it with any degree of immediacy. But his case is rare. Most of what passes as the literature of mean streets has been composed by well-intentioned respectable gentlemen to whose lives a mean street has no more relevance than a mummy to an Egyptologist. James and Conrad each approached the depiction of London's lower depths with that incorruptible integrity we have come to expect of them, but theirs was the appalled and generally humourless fascination of the foreign explorer. Writers like George Moore and Hubert Crackanthorpe made genuine attempts to verbalize on behalf of the inarticulate, but readable though their best work remains, it has been well said of them that they 'retain a feeling of having been translated from the French originals'. Artists as disparate as Gissing and Orwell have fled from respectability into the working class as if into the arms of a benign goddess, without grasping the simple proposition that the working class is neither more virtuous nor less than any other; it is poorer, that is all. The result has been the neglect of the largest single group in the community. Doomed to being either sentimentalized by the guiltwracked or stigmatized by the pietistic, the urban masses in English literature almost never appear as themselves, but only as something which might be turned into something else, either the saintly redeemers of Orwell's dreams or the avenging mob of Dickens' nightmares.

But there does exist an authentic literature of the urban poor, small in extent perhaps, but intense in effect. Arthur Morrison in particular, in *A Child of the Jago*, *Tales of Mean Streets* and *The Hole in the Wall*, spared his readers so little in his account of how the slum-dweller lived his life and saw the world that there are moments when the brutalized characters in their stunted surroundings become too awful to read about. Indeed Morrison did his job so convincingly that social engineers since have been misled into thinking that because violence and criminality came out of the Jago, then the Jago can produce nothing but violence and criminality. The conclusion is comically false, and Morrison went out of his way to say so, insisting that brutality and crime were only two aspects among many of working-class life and by no means the most dominant. Nor were they exclusive to the working class; there is after all some kinship between the man who shoots a few grouse before having his lunch and his contemporary who squashes a few bedbugs before going to sleep. Most of the residents of Morrison's mean streets, housed in pigsties at the very apogee of Empire, aspired to graduate from the bugs to the grouse, figuratively speaking, by lawful means, and often succeeded. Virtue resided cheek by jowl with vice, sapience often shared a bed with doltishness, an intermingling perfectly defined by a passage in the reminiscences of Poplar-born H. M. Tomlinson, who remembered corners and byways avoided by all except the doctor and the venturesome, where a policeman's helmet might be seen in the gutter on the morning following Saturday night. There it stayed. Nobody would touch it. Meddle with the Law?

The point about that helmet is that somebody must have put it there, and the interest of a book like *The Hooligan Nights* is that it shows us the world through the eyes of the culprit. Clarence Rook's approach is unusual in that it is almost entirely free of the sanctimony of its day. Dispensing gleefully with the conventional honour-among-thieves cant, Rook implies by the studied detachment of his view that there is precious little honour to be found anywhere in the big city, which although untrue, is a useful corrective to the belief prevalent at the time among divines and the genteel crusaders of the good-works brigade that there is no Englishman so ignoble that he will not respond to the blandishments of an illuminated text or a free bowl of soup; one of the Hooligan's most passionate beliefs is that the magistrates who try his misdemeanours are no more to be trusted as receptacles of the law than the thieves on whom they sit in judgment. At this point Rook comes perilously close to the once fashionable quackery that we are all criminals together, that Society, having created an auspicious criminal environment, is itself the criminal. Whether Rook really believed this is impossible to decide without knowing a great deal more about him than we do, but he certainly affected to believe it in *The Hooligan Nights*, revelling in the relentless felonies of his hero, striving to scandalize the custodians of received morality with his chronicle of moral turpitude unredeemed by so much as a glimmer of compunction. And as if to make sure we do not overlook the sardonic nature of the enterprise, Rook time and again leads us up the garden path, gulling us into the expectation of some touch of gallantry, only to thump us all the harder with the climactic revelation of sheer rottenness, as in the episode entitled 'Honest Employment', where the slavey who has allowed herself to become an accessory to the Hooligan's crimes loses her post and yet 'never fingered a bleed'n farden'.

In fact, Rook's apparent equanimity in the face of the Hooligan's callousness is almost too well sustained. In the episode 'Class!', the criminal shrugs his shoulders at the suggestion that perhaps one of his victims might have died; in 'The Coming of Love' the episode is shadowed by the appalling cruelty of the injury to the bull terrier; even when the Hooligan appears to be expressing some sort of moral opinion, as in his disapproval of prostitution, we soon realize that he is saying the right things for the wrong reasons, and that his objections are rooted not in some garbled ideal of romance but in his discovery that the prostitute is one of his most formidable professional rivals, 'for when the toff has been picked clean by the female thief there is very little left for the Lambeth lad'. It would take a moral imbecile not to be repelled by much of this sort of business, yet Rook offers us no sign that he is shocked or angry. Such things happen because they happen, and the world can hardly be disgusted by them, otherwise it would have taken steps long ago. Instead it is content to jog along contiguous with the most hair-raising lawlessness; when, in 'Playing for the Pocket' Rook goes off for an assignation with his criminal friend, there is deep mockery in the exactitude with which he locates the thieves' kitchen for which he is bound, reminding us that it lies 'in one of the small streets which run behind the place where the Archbishop of Canterbury gives garden parties'.

There are surprisingly few lapses from this detachment, and these are brought about through three agencies which,

Introduction

unfortunate though they may be so far as the artistic unity of the book is concerned, do help us fill out the shadowy lineaments of the man responsible for them. One of Rook's occasional tendencies is to wallow in the bogus pantheism which disfigures so many popular texts of the period. Each age has its own brand of fustian, and in Rook's day it was considered obligatory to give the reader periodic reminders of the author's poetic credentials. Rook's bathetic raptures about the Thames at night which open the chapter called 'Politics' are a disastrous intrusion recalling the worst excesses of Jerome K. Jerome, and it is interesting to compare Rook's 'fairy river spanned by bridges of gossamer' and 'the silver path of the moon upon the river break into ten thousand diamonds', with the awful paroxysms of Jerome's Night, which, not content with having 'folded her black wings above the darkening world', then 'gently lays her hands upon our fevered brow and turns our little tear-stained face up to hers'. An entity which possesses hands AND wings sounds more formidable than anything the bandersnatch or the jabberwock could offer, and it must be said for Rook that he never quite sinks to such depths.

A second and more damaging discord is struck when the narrative drifts from its documentary detachment into the contrivances of plotmaking; so marked is this impression that it is fictional parallels rather than actuality which the episodes of the Hooligan's career evoke. Rook opens the proceedings with a brave flourish which suggests that he knew he would be accused of gilding the lily. But in so modestly denying his status as a novelist, he sounds very much like a man who protests too much. Much closer to the truth is Professor P. J. Keating, who, in selecting three sections of *The Hooligan Nights* for his anthology *Working-class Stories of the 1890s*, writes:

We cannot, of course, fully accept Rook's disclaimer. The principal incidents in many of the sketches are too slickly presented for them to pass as unadulterated reporting, and we are often conscious that they belong generically to the age-old literature of roguery.

Time and again the adventures of young Hooligan Alf remind us of similar exploits in other, fictitious contexts. His apprenticeship as a fanlight-jumper is a direct crib from the episode in *Oliver Twist* where the young hero is obliged to become assistant to Bill Sikes; when Alf describes how the Salvation Army has 'bin tryin' to get 'old o' me', a picture suddenly springs to mind of Shaw's Bill Walker nine years later informing Major Barbara that 'there aint no such thing as a saoul. You never seen it' (the suggestion that Shaw might have been influenced by Rook's idea is not quite so farfetched as it sounds, as we will see). As for the episode of 'The Burglar and the Baby', in which the Hooligan is distracted from his calling by the plight of a child, it would be interesting to know if Damon Runyon had come across *The Hooligan Nights* when he wrote *Butch Minds the Baby*, where the only real difference to Rook's story is that this time the burglar is impeded by his own child instead of his victim's. In all these episodes there is a strong impression of a tale being told rather than of the facts being reported, and this sense becomes overwhelming at least twice, in the episode where Alf is being chased through the streets and eludes his pursuers by pretending to be one of them, a scenario better suited to the slapstick of Buster Keaton or Laurel and Hardy than to an apparently sober account of the London criminal life; and the story of young Maggots, who resolves the complexities of his own love life by arranging a tryst at the same time at the same place with two of his followers, and then enjoys the fight which follows. At such moments

Introduction

Rook may insist on his passive role as vociferously as he pleases without convincing us.

His third failing, at once the most human and the most revealing of all, is that as the melodrama unfolds, he cannot resist the temptation to take the centre of the stage. At first he struggles to remain impersonal, an amused chimera stalking the alleys of a vanished London underworld, although from that moonlit moment when he follows Alf into the stable where the stolen meat was stashed, his personality begins to obtrude; he becomes from that point our surrogate self, the emissary of the daylight world daring to step down into the dangers of the Hooligan's minatory principality. But for a while he resists at least the temptation to announce his authorial descent; in these earlier episodes he might indeed be the mere observer he claims, the journalistic messenger boy running errands for his master, the publisher Grant Richards. But steadily the compulsion grows stronger for the narrator to assert his intellectual primacy. In 'The Boot-trick and Others' he gives us a sharp reminder that we are after all in the hands of an experienced professional romancer when he draws a facetious analogy between the burglar obliged by hard times to stoop to the expediency of dog-stealing, and the novelist who 'frequently finds it profitable to fill up odd time with journalism'. In the chapter called 'Politics' he becomes much bolder by hinting that not only is he a bona fide literary artist but the only one capable of winning the Hooligan's confidence. Alf makes a contemptuous remark about a certain 'Orfer, wrote about fings in the papers', and we know from the unheard tone of his voice that we are to understand that only Rook could ever have succeeded in compiling the volume which now rests in the reader's hands. The seventh veil is finally lifted in 'Strange Dwellings', where Rook emerges in full costume and trappings, from the servant announcing a mysterious visitor in the hall, to the fire burning in the study grate; here is a room fit for the purple patch and the furrowed brow. At this point the author has invaded the world of his characters so successfully that we can no longer assess his intentions without knowing certain things about him. In order to gauge the degree to which a book of adventure has fulfilled its promise, we need only to watch its hero moving through the ramifications of the plot. Certainly by the time Alf arrives at Rook's door we know him well. But this is no longer enough – for *The Hooligan Nights* has two heroes, and the other one is Clarence Rook.

Which raises a difficulty. We must try to deduce whether the book is reportage or contrivance, whether the social document of Rook's prefatory disclaimer, or the latest episode of what Professor Keating has memorably defined as the literature of roguery. And in order to make our informed guesses, we have to get to know Rook at least as intimately as he claims to know Alf. But how? Few authors of the period can have vanished as effectively as Rook; the curious investigator, resorting with excusable complacency to the usual volumes of reference and reminiscence which record the backgrounds, careers, and eventual fates of so many forgotten Victorian and Edwardian lions, is suddenly brought up short; index after index discloses nothing more enlightening than a hiatus between 'Ronsard' and 'Rossetti'. It is as though Clarence Rook had never really existed at all, and his name a mere pseudonymous subterfuge indulged in by some timorous bellettrist anxious to conceal an unfortunate familiarity with the low life. Perhaps it was Grant Richards himself who did the deed; after all, he wrote at least two readable books published under his own name.

However, persistent pursuit reveals that Rook, if not a figment of Richards' imagination, was at any rate one of those elusive residents of Grub Street who survive only vicariously in the destinies of other men. Even this curious, pathetic life, lived as it were at one remove from its own reality, is hardly prolific, and the researcher has to be lucky as well as assiduous if he is to catch a glimpse of Rook flashing across the literary landscape into the fast-lengthening shadows of Edwardian journalistic history, like a kingfisher at dusk. What renders his case more exasperating than ever is that the little evidence which does exist tantalizes us with lavish praise and half-formulated intimations which somehow leave us knowing less rather than more.

A typical example is Edward Verrall Lucas, who, in a volume of autobiography called *Reading, Writing and Remembering*, suddenly bestows on the Rook researcher that stabbing delight of sudden recognition generally defined as serendipity. Lucas is describing one of his many posts, as contributor to the 'By the Way' column in a long-since vanished London newspaper called *The Globe*, in the course of which he makes a passing reference which compounds rather than resolves the mystery: '... Clarence Rook, a writer who never fulfilled his many talents'. Lucas omits to say what those talents were, or why Rook failed to fulfil them, but his remark at least tells us something about the kind of journalistic work which Rook was considered to be capable of performing. 'By the Way' was a typical journalistic feature of its period; by a fortunate coincidence we have been left a brief but graphic account of how it operated and what it required of the men who contributed to it. A journalistic beginner, later to become one of the most prolific novelists of the century, has written:

There was an evening paper called 'The Globe'. It was 105 years old and was printed on – so help me – pink paper. It carried on its front page a humorous column entitled 'By the Way'. There was quite a bit of prestige attached to doing it.

In another context on the same theme, P. G. Wodehouse elaborates:

> The column itself was an extraordinary affair. You would quote something from the morning paper and then you'd make some little comment on it. It was always the same type of joke.

The duties of contributors to 'By the Way' were intense but hardly arduous; Wodehouse says that his presence at *The Globe* was required only from 10 a.m. to noon each day. Such posts have always been popular with journalists of Rook's type, whose temperament yearns for the liberations of the free-lance life without its financial uncertainties. Wodehouse joined 'By the Way' in 1902, and says that Lucas pre-dated him by a year or two. This would place Rook at *The Globe* around 1900, not so very long after the publication of *The Hooligan Nights*, but several years earlier than his second book of metropolitan sketches, *London Sidelights*, published by Arnold in 1908; evidently Rook evolved into mastery of a specialization later performed by writers like Thomas Burke and Stephen Graham.

Very much more revealing than Lucas is, of all people, Bernard Shaw, who approves so vehemently of Rook that he actually takes the trouble to write to his official biographer, Archibald Henderson, warning him not to invite unfavourable comparisons. The point arose in 1905 when Henderson, researching Shaw's protean past in preparation for his biography, came across references to an American publication called *The Chap Book*, which in 1896 had carried a piece on Shaw of unusual percipience. The first reference to this publication can be found in a letter from Shaw to Ellen Terry on 21 September 1896, written on an Underground train, hence the address: 'Smoke, fog, filth, and joggle-joggle'. These were early days in the Shaw-

Introduction

Terry epistolary romance, and Shaw was still very much preoccupied with the challenge of presenting to Miss Terry a view of himself commensurate with his own assessment. He writes:

> I will send you an account of myself presently; there is one coming out in an American magazine. If the interviewer, who is a very clever fellow, hits me off, you shall have the magazine.

That Shaw is referring to Rook is confirmed by a second letter, to the other woman in his life, Charlotte Payne-Townsend, written on 18 November 1896, from Fitzroy Square:

> I send you a copy of 'The Chap Book' with a caricature of me by Max Beerbohm and an interview by Clarence Rook.

Thus, within a period of two months, Shaw is using Rook as a letter of recommendation to the two most important women in his life. Any lingering doubt that he thought well of Rook is dispelled finally by his letter to Henderson on 3 January 1905:

> The reference in N.Y. Bookman to an article dealing with my youth and early manhood must be to an article 'George Bernard Shaw' by Clarence Rook (published by H. S. Stone and Co; of Chicago) for November, 1896. This is one of the best things of the kind ever done about me. (Copy enclosed).

A month later, writing from Adelphi Terrace, Shaw advises his would-be biographer:

> Unless you can show me in the context of my time, as a member of a very interesting crowd, you will fail to produce the only thing that makes biography tolerable. Observe, I am not treating you as a smart young journalist. Clarence Rook can beat you at that probably.

It was a warning which Henderson presumably took to heart; Shaw, the last great Grub Street journalist of the age, was rarely so lavish with his praises. The fact that the scorn for his biographers with which he lacerated the likes of Frank Harris, Winston Churchill, Professor O'Bolger, and Henry Charles Duffin was on this occasion withheld, says much for Rook, whose interview, entitled 'Nine Answers', includes the now famous remarks by Shaw that 'in 1876 London was not ripe for Me' and 'I was not un-educated; but unfortunately what I knew was exactly what the educated Englishman did not know; and what he knew I either didn't know or didn't believe'.

There are at least two other glimpses of Rook worth mentioning. As recently as 1975 he turned up as a con-tributor to an anthology of mystery stories, of which his item, 'The Stir Outside the Cafe Royal', features a lady sleuth with the unfortunate name of Miss Van Snoop. This story was first published in Harmsworth's Magazine for September 1898, so perhaps Rook's experiences at the hands of the Hooligan gave him a taste for the retailing of petty larceny. But the most tantalizing reference of all is surely the one made by Grant Richards himself in that curiosity of an autobiography, *Author Hunting*, in which, after indulging in some candour regarding the genesis of his publishing house in 1896 on a capital of £1,400, he says, apropos Shaw's interest in prizefighting:

> Having been to fights about half a dozen times in my life, I am all for the referee being kept out of the ring. But obvi-ously I cannot set up as one whose opinion is worth a tinker's curse. I have been taken to a fight by the Hooligan of Clarence Rook's *Hooligan Nights* – a fight at which he him-self was beaten – that took place in a railway arch somewhere down Lambeth way.

This must be a reference to the fight in the chapter 'All for

Introduction

Her' in which the Hooligan is outpointed by the more
skilful Ginger and later reverses the decision on the cobbles.
The corroboration suggests that perhaps after all Rook
was being frank when he says that his introduction to the
exploits of Alf was effected by Richards himself.

Who then, was Clarence Rook? We know for certain
that at any rate between 1896 and 1908 he practised the
craft of casual journalism with enough adroitness to satisfy
not only the greatest literary figure of the period but also
the privateers of pulp journalism. But what manner of
man was he? And more to the point in the context of the
Hooligan, what manner of man did he believe the next
man should be? Is Rook genuinely indifferent to young
Alf's brutalized sensibilities? Or is he deriding more
fastidious professional rivals by rubbing their noses in Alf's
irredeemable venality? Does he find those venalities
regrettable but consider that the architectural and sanitary
shortcomings of Lambeth life at the turn of the century
excuse them? (Those who subscribe to this theory will no
doubt enjoy being refuted by the autobiography of Alf's
contemporary from St George's Road, Lambeth – Charlie
Chaplin). Had Rook himself lived the life of reckless in-
discipline depicted in the pages of *The Hooligan Nights*,
and had he perhaps been sought out to do the job by Grant
Richards for that very reason?

It would seem not. A Death Certificate entered at St
George, Hanover Square, in the sub-district of Belgrave in
the county of London, tells us that Clarence Henry Rook,
journalist, of 52, Tregunter Road, Kensington, born 1862,
died on 23 December 1915 of 'Paralysis, bed sores and
exhaustion', with his wife Clare in attendance. We know
also that in 1893, while living in St Petersburgh Place,
Bayswater, Rook had made a will, and that after his death
his wife inherited the sum of £1301. Neither his addresses
nor the proximity of his wife nor the amount of money he

left her would suggest that Rook ever remotely approached the kind of squalor he depicts in *The Hooligan Nights*. And yet – why would an apparently healthy young man make out a will at the age of 31? Was this the year he married Clare? Or does it represent a juncture in his life when he discovered something about his own expectations which inclined him to morbidity? The Death Certificate registers one other fact about Rook, which is that at the time he died he had been suffering for the past 26 years from Locomotor Ataxy. Now the medical books are inclined to leave the impression that Locomotor Ataxy, in which the victim loses muscular control, was a euphemism for venereal disease: 'associated with syphilis, treatment as for syphilis'. Perhaps then, Rook, the 'honest citizen, paying rates and taxes, living in a house, serving on juries', had in his youth conducted some costly transaction with one of the Lizzies and Alices who so doted on young Alf. But what of *The Hooligan Nights*? Are we to take it as a social document, or as a flourish of literary artifice in the wake of more prestigious gestures in the same direction? (Maugham's *Liza of Lambeth* had appeared amid considerable controversy in September 1897). Did the Hooligan tread the pavements of the real Lambeth south of the river, or only of the spectral one inside Clarence Rook's head? Did he write the book as a novelist – or merely because he found it 'profitable to fill up odd time with journalism'? As to that, the reader must decide for himself.

Benny Green
1979

Introduction to the 1899 edition

This is neither a novel, nor in any sense a work of imagination. Whatever value or interest the following chapters possess must come from the fact that their hero has a real existence. I have tried to set forth, as far as possible in his own words, certain scenes from the life of a young criminal with whom I chanced to make acquaintance, a boy who has grown up in the midst of those who gain their living on the crooked, who takes life and its belongings as he finds them, and is not in the least ashamed of himself.

My introduction to young Alf came about in this wise: Mr Grant Richards, the publisher, one day showed me some sheets of manuscript which he said might interest me. They did. They contained certain confessions and revelations of a boy who professed to be a leader of Hooligans. But what interested me most was the engaging personality behind these confessions, and I asked Mr Richards to bring us together. A meeting was arranged, and I was not disappointed. This led to other meetings, during which I became so interested in young Alf that it occurred to me to place him on record, thinking that you would not be unwilling to have a photograph of the young man who walks to and fro in your midst, ready to pick your pocket, rifle your house, and even bash you in a dark corner if it is made worth his while. For young Alf is not unique. His views are the views of a section of Londoners that would suffice to people – say Canterbury. They live in certain more or less well-defined areas, but their business quarter is the metropolis with its suburbs, and the warfare that they wage is constant and pitiless.

I do not know that there is any particular moral to be drawn from this book, and in any case I shall leave you to draw it for yourself. But please do not accuse it of being immoral. When the Daily Chronicle *published portions of the history of young Alf early in the year the editor received numerous complaints from well-meaning people who protested that I had painted the life of a criminal in alluring colours. They forgot, I presume, that young Alf was a study in reality, and that in real life the villain does not invariably come to grief before he has come of age. Poetic justice demands that young Alf should be very unhappy; as a matter of fact, he is nothing of the sort. And when you come to think of it, he has had a livelier time than the average clerk on a limited number of shillings a week. He does not know what it is to be bored. Every day has its interests, and every day has its possibility of the unexpected, which is just what the steady honest worker misses. He need not consider appearances, being indeed more concerned for his disappearances, he has ample leisure, and each job he undertakes has the excitement of novelty and the promise of immediate and usually generous reward. It would, I think, be very difficult to persuade young Alf that honesty is the best policy. I am not responsible for the constitution of the universe; and if under the present conditions of life a Lambeth boy can get more fun by going sideways than by going straight, I cannot help it. I do not commend the ways of my young friend, or even apologize for them. I simply set him before you as a fact that must be dealt with. Young Alf has interested me hugely, and I trust he will not bore you.*

Clarence Rook

I

Young Alf

On this particular occasion we met by appointment at the
Elephant and Castle. He had a kip in the vicinity; that is,
there was a bed, which was little better than a board, in
one of those places where your welcome extends from sun-
set to sunrise; and to this he had recurred for some five
nights in succession. For some reason or other he was unwilling to conduct me to his precise address for the current
week. So we met, by appointment, where the omnibuses
converge and separate to their destinations in all parts of
South London, on the kerbstone at the Elephant.

I was in a sense a pilgrim. Good Americans, when they
come to London, may be seen peering in Bolt Court and
eating their dinner at the Cheshire Cheese. I was bound on
an expedition to the haunts of a more recent celebrity than
Dr Johnson. My destination was Irish Court and the Lamb
and Flag. For in the former Patrick Hooligan lived a portion of his ill-spent life, and gave laws and a name to his
followers; in the latter, the same Patrick was to be met
night by night, until a higher law than his own put a
period to his rule.

Moreover, my companion was one on whom a portion at
least of Patrick Hooligan's mantle had fallen; a young man
– he was scarcely more than seventeen – who held by the
Hooligan tradition, and controlled a gang of boys who
made their living by their wits, and were ready for any
devilry if you assured them of even an inadequate reward.

Young Alf – this is not the name by which the constable
on point duty at the Elephant mentions him to his col-
league who comes along from St George's Road – young Alf

was first at the meeting-place. He had, he explained, an evening to spare, and there were lots of worse places than the Elephant.

Young Alf beckoned; and while I hovered on the kerb, watching the charging 'buses, the gliding trams, and the cabs that twinkled their danger signals, he had plunged into the traffic and slithered through, dodging 'buses and skirting cabs without a turn of the head. He went through the traffic with a quiet, confident twist of the body, as a fish whisks its way through scattered rocks, touching nothing, but always within a hair's-breadth of collision. On the other side he awaited me, careless, and indeed a little contemptuous; and together we made our way towards Bethlehem Hospital, and thence in the direction of Lambeth Walk.

As we swung round a corner I noticed a man in the doorway of a shop – a bald-headed man with spectacles, and in his shirt-sleeves, though the night was chilly.

'Ain't caught yer yet?' was the remark that young Alf flung at him, without turning his head half a point.

'You take a lot o' catchin', you do,' retorted the man.

Young Alf looked round at me. I expected to hear him laugh, or chuckle, or at the least seem amused. And it came upon me with something of a shock that I had never, so far as I could remember, seen him laugh. His face was grave, tense, eager, as always.

'That's a fence,' he said. 'I lived there when I was a nipper, wiv my muvver – and a accerabat.'

'Was that when—' I began.

'Don't talk,' he muttered, for we had emerged upon Lambeth Walk. The Walk, as they term it to whom Lambeth Walk is Bond Street, the promenade, the place to shop, to lounge, to listen to music and singing, to steal, if opportunity occur, to make love, and not infrequently to fight.

2

The moon was up, and struggling intermittently through clouds; this was probably one of the reasons why young Alf allowed himself an evening of leisure. But Lambeth Walk had no need of a moon: it was Saturday night, and the Walk was aflare with gas and naphtha, which lighted up the street from end to end, and emphasized the gloom of the narrow openings which gave entrance to the network of courts between the Walk and the railway arches behind it.

The whole social life of a district was concentrated in the two hundred yards of roadway, which was made even narrower by the double line of barrows which flanked it. There was not a well-dressed person to be seen, scarcely a passably clean one. But there was none of the hopeless poverty one might have seen at the same hour in Piccadilly; and no one looked in the least bored. Business and pleasure jostled one another. Every corner had its side-show to which you must turn your attention for a moment in the intervals of haggling over your Sunday's dinner. Here at this corner is a piano-organ, with small children dancing wildly for the mere fun of the thing. There is no dancing for coppers in the Walk. At the next corner is a miniature shooting gallery; the leather-lunged proprietor shouts with well-assumed joy when a crack shot makes the bell ring for the third time, and bears off the cocoa-nut.

'Got 'im again!' he bawls delightedly, as though he lived only to give cocoa-nuts away to deserving people.

Hard by the bland owner of a hand-cart is recommending an 'unfallible cure for toothache' to a perverse and unbelieving audience. As we pass we hear him saying,

'I've travelled 'underds of miles in my time, ladies and gentlemen – all the world over; but this I will say – and let him deny it that can, and I maintain he can't – and that is this, that never in the 'ole course of my experience have

3

I met so sceptical a lot of people as you Londoners. You ain't to be took in. You know—'

But young Alf was making his way through the crowd, and I hurried after him.

Literature, too, by the barrowful; paper covers with pictures that hit you between the eyes and made you blink. And music! 'Words and music. Four a penny, and all different.'

You may buy anything and everything in the Walk – caps, canaries, centre-bits, oranges, toffee, saucepans, to say nothing of fried fish, butchers' meat, and green stuff; everything, in fact, that you could require to make you happy. And a pervading cheerfulness is the note of the Walk.

On that Saturday evening there were probably more people in Lambeth Walk who made their living on the crooked than in any other street of the same length in London. Yet the way of transgressors seemed a cheerful one. Everybody was good-humoured, and nobody was more than reasonably drunk.

Lower down we came to the meat stalls, over which the butchers were shouting the praises of prime joints. As we passed, a red-faced man with sandy whiskers suddenly dropped his voice to the level of ordinary conversation.

'You ain't selling no meat to-night, ain't you?' He said, cocking a knowing eye at my companion.

Young Alf glanced quickly at the butcher, and then round at me.

'I'll tell you about that presently,' he said, in answer to my look of inquiry.

''Ere we are,' said young Alf, a few moments later, as we turned suddenly from the glaring, shouting, seething Walk, redolent of gas, naphtha, second-hand shoe-leather, and fried fish, into a dark entrance. Dimly I could see that the entrance broadened a few yards down into a court of

4

about a dozen feet in width. No light shone from any of the
windows, no gas-lamp relieved the gloom. The court ran
from the glare of the street into darkness and mystery.

Young Alf hesitated a moment or two in the shadow.
Then he said:

'Look 'ere, you walk froo' – straight on; it ain't far, and
I'll be at the uvver end to meet you.'

'Why don't you come with me?' I asked. I could see
that he was looking me up and down critically.

'Not down there,' he said; 'they'd think I was narkin'.
You look a dam sight too much like a split to-night.' Then
I remembered that he had been keeping a little ahead of
me ever since we had met at the Elephant and Castle. I had
unthinkingly neglected to adapt my dress in any way to
the occasion, and in consequence was subjecting my friend
to uneasiness and possible annoyance.

I expressed my regret, and, buttoning my coat, started
down the court as young Alf melted into the crowd in
Lambeth Walk. It was not a pretty court. The houses
were low, with narrow doorways and windows that showed
no glimmer of light. Heaps of garbage assailed the feet and
the nose. Not a living soul was to be seen until I had
nearly reached the other end, and could just discern the
form of young Alf leaning against one of the posts at the
exit of the court. Then suddenly two women in white
aprons sprang into view from nowhere, gave a cry, and
stood watching me from a doorway.

'They took you for a split,' said young Alf, as we met at
the end of the court. 'I know'd they would. 'Ello, Alice!'

A girl stood in the deep shadow of the corner house. Her
head was covered by a shawl, and I could not see her face,
but her figure showed youth and a certain grace.

''Ello!' she said, without moving.

'When you goin' to get married?' asked young Alf.

'When it comes,' replied the girl softly.

The voice that falls like velvet on your ear and lingers in your memory is rare. Wendell Holmes says somewhere that he had heard but two perfect speaking voices, and one of them belonged to a German chambermaid. The softest and most thrilling voice I ever heard I encountered at the corner of one of the lowest slums in London.

Young Alf was apparently unaffected by it, for, having thus accorded the courtesy due to an acquaintance, he whipped round swiftly to me and said;

'Where them women's standing is where Pat Hooligan lived, 'fore he was pinched.'

It stood no higher than the houses that elbowed it, and had nothing to distinguish it from its less notable neighbours. But if a Hooligan boy prayed at all, he would pray with his face toward that house half-way down Irish Court.

'And next door – this side,' continued young Alf, 'that's where me and my muvver kipped when I was a nipper.'

The tone of pride was unmistakable, for the dwelling-place of Patrick Hooligan enshrines the ideal towards which the Ishmaelites of Lambeth are working; and, as I afterwards learned, young Alf's supremacy over his comrades was sealed by his association with the memory of the Prophet.

'This way,' said young Alf.

The girl stood, still motionless, in the shadow, with one hand clasping the shawl that enveloped her head. Here was stark solitude and dead silence, with a background of shouting, laughter, rifle-shots, and the tramp of myriad feet from the Walk thirty yards away. I hesitated, in the hope of hearing her voice again. But I was not to hear it a second time for many days; and she remained silent and motionless as we plunged again into obscurity.

Under the railway arches it was as black as pitch.

"Sh!' said young Alf warningly, as I stumbled. It was

6

too dark to see the lithe, sinewy hand that he placed on my own for my guidance.

In a few seconds we had turned – as my nose gave evidence – into a stable-yard. Upon one corner the moon shone, bringing a decrepit van into absurd prominence.

''Ere's where me and my pal was – up to last week,' said young Alf in a whisper.

He slipped across to a dark corner, and I followed. A stable dog barked, and then, as we stood still, lapsed into silence.

'Got a match?' said young Alf.

I handed him a box of matches, and he struck one, shading it with his hands so skilfully that no glimmer fell anywhere but on the latch of a door.

'Awright,' he muttered, as the door swung back noiselessly. Then he turned and put his face close to mine. 'If anybody wants to know anyfink, you swank as you want to take the room. See?'

The stairs were steep and in bad repair, for they creaked horribly under my feet. But young Alf as he ascended in front of me was inaudible, and I thought I had lost him and myself, until I ran into him at the top.

From utter blackness we turned into a room flooded by moonlight, a room in no way remarkable to the sight, but such a room as you may see when you are house-hunting in the suburbs, ascend to the top floor of a desirable residence, and are told that this is a servant's bedroom. The walls were papered; it had a single window through which the moonlight was streaming, and it was quite empty, save for something lying in the corner of the window – apparently a horse-cloth.

'This is where we was, me and 'im,' said young Alf. 'There's anuvver room across the landing.'

'Who was him?' I asked.

Young Alf walked over to the window, looked down into

the yard below, and made no reply. There were things here and there that he would not tell me.

'Why did you leave?' I resumed. 'It seems a convenient sort of place to live in. Quiet enough, wasn't it?'

'Well, it was like this,' he said. 'Me and 'im was making snide coin; least 'e was making it, and I was planting it – 'ere, there, and everywhere. See?'

'Made it in this room? How did he make it?'

''E'd never show me the way. But it didn't take him long. Well, we got planting it a bit too thick, 'cos there was more'n one on the same fake, and the cops come smellin' about. So we did a scoot. Time enough it was.'

'Smelling,' I said; 'I should think they did. It's enough to knock you down.'

'I fought I noticed somefink,' he said sharply, and in an instant he had pounced upon the object in the corner, and from underneath the horse-cloth drew a joint of meat, which at once proclaimed itself as the origin of the awful stench.

'Wonder how that got left 'ere?' said young Alf, as he opened the window gently and heaved the joint into the yard below.

'Better leave the window open,' I said as he was about to close it.

'Didn't I never tell you,' he said, 'how we waxed things up for that butcher as come down to the Walk? Battersea he come from.'

I had not heard the story, and said so.

'It was that what give the show away,' he said. 'You 'eard what that butcher said jest now?'

I nodded.

He leaned against the window sill, and, with one eye on the stable-yard, told me the story.

'It was Friday night last week,' he began, 'and me and two uvvers was coming along the Walk, down where the

butchers are. There was one butcher there that I tumbled
was a stranger soon as I ketch sight of 'is dial. He wasn't
selling 'is meat over-quick, 'cos 'alf the time he was neck-
ing four-ale in the pub 'cross the way. He'd got 'is joints
laid out beautiful on a sort of barrer. Well, we 'ung about,
watchin' 'im go 'cross the road and come back again, and
presently I says to the uvvers, 'That bloke don't seem to
be doin' no trade worf mentionin'. Let's, 'elp 'im.' Well,
the uvver boys didn't want asking more'n once to do a
poor bloke a good turn, so we just scatters and waits a bit
till the butcher went 'cross the way again for 'is wet; nor
we didn't 'ave to wait long neither. Soon as he goes into
the pub we nips round and shifts his old barrer, and 'fore
you could say knife we had it froo the arches and in the
stable-yard here. We got the meat upstairs, and then we
run the empty barrer outside, and left it standin' in
Paradise Street, where it couldn't do no one any 'arm.'

'But didn't anyone see you shift the barrow?' I asked.

''Ow was they to know we wasn't in the employment of
the butcher?' he retorted. 'Besides, the uvver butchers
wasn't likely to make a fuss. They didn't want no strangers
comin' and interferin' wiv their pitch.'

'And did you see any more of the butcher?' I inquired.

'What do you fink?' he said. 'Presently we went back
again to the Walk, and it wasn't 'alf a minute before we
saw the butcher tearin' up and down lookin' for his barrer.
Of course nobody 'adn't seen anyfink of it. Then he started
on the pubs, and went into every pub in the Walk askin'
after his barrer. He had a lot of wet, but he didn't find his
barrer, nor no meat neither. We went into one or two of
the pubs after 'im, and gave 'im a lot of symperfy, jest
abart as much as he could do wiv. One of the boys says:
'Sims to me your legs 'ave taken to walkin' again,
guv'nor.' And the butcher couldn't 'ardly keep 'is 'air on.
Then anuvver of the boys says he never was so sorry for

anyfink in all his life. Come all the way from the Angel up at Islington, 'e 'ad, purpose to get a prime joint at the new butcher's in the Walk. That butcher's joints was the fair talk round Upper Street way, he says. What 'e'd say to the missus when 'e come home empty-'anded he didn't know, he says.

'Then I chipped in.

' "Well, guv'nor," I says, "they tell me you've beat all them uvver butchers to-night. You've cleared out all your stock 'fore anyone else, 'aven't you? And you ain't given none of it away, neither."

'Wiv that he fair got 'is monkey up, and he went off down the Walk ragin' and roarin'; and me and the uvver boys went back to where we'd planted the meat. There was meat goin' cheap that night down our way – less than cawst-price, wiv no error. And some of them butchers wasn't quite so pleased as they fort they was, when they found legs of mutton sellin' at frippence a pound.'

'And what became of the unfortunate butcher?' I asked.

'Last thing I see of him he'd had more'n enough already. And then he got into a 'ouse – not what you might call a resky 'ome – and there they put him to sleep, and went froo his pockets, and pitched him out in the mornin', skinned – feer skinned 'e was. The cops found 'is barrer next mornin', and wheeled it off. But the butcher never showed 'is dial again in the Walk. Bit too 'ot.'

'Rather rough on the butcher, wasn't it?' I suggested. 'But you probably didn't think of that.'

His eyes glanced quickly from mine to the yard below, and back to mine again, and for a moment – perhaps it was the moonlight that caught his face and gave it a weird twist – but for the moment he looked like a rat.

'I got meself to fink abart,' he said; 'and if I went finkin' abart uvver people I shouldn't be no good at this game. I wonder which of them silly young blokes it was forgot that leg of mutton I chucked outer winder.'

He peered over the sill, and the dog began barking again. But the step in the lane outside passed on. And young Alf turned again to me and expounded his philosophy of life.

'Look 'ere,' he said, 'if you see a fing you want, you just go and take it wivout any 'anging abart. If you 'ang abart you draw suspicion, and you get lagged for loiterin' wiv intent to commit a felony or some dam nonsense like that. Go for it, strite. P'r'aps it's a 'awse and cart you see as'll do you fine. Jump up and drive away as 'ard as you can, and ten to one nobody'll say anyfink. They'll think it's your own prop'ty. But 'ang around, and you mit jest as well walk into the next cop you see, and arst 'im to 'and you your stretch. See? You got to look after yourself; and it ain't your graft to look after anyone else, nor it ain't likely that anybody else'd look after you – only the cops. See?'

A cloud came over the moon, and threw the room and the yard outside into darkness. Young Alf became a dim shadow against the window.

'Time we was off,' he said.

He shut down the window softly, and, by the shaded light of a match with which I supplied him, led me to the door and down the stairs. The dog was awake and alert, and barked noisily, though young Alf's step would not have broken an egg or caused a hare to turn in its sleep. He protested in a whisper against my inability to tread a stair without bringing the house about my ears. But the yard outside was empty, and no one but the dog seemed aware of our presence. Young Alf was bound, he said, for the neighbourhood of Westminster Bridge, but he walked with me down to Vauxhall Station through a network of dim and silent streets.

I inquired of his plans for the night, and he explained
that there was a bit of a street-fight in prospect. The Drury
Lane boys were coming across the bridge, and had engaged to meet the boys from Lambeth Walk at a coffee-
stall on the other side. Then one of the Lambeth boys
would make to one of the Drury Lane boys a remark
which cannot be printed, but never fails to send the monkey of a Drury Lane boy a considerable way up the pole.
Whereafter the Drury Lane boys would fall upon the
Lambeth boys, and the Lambeth boys would give them
what for.

As we came under the gas-lamps of Upper Kennington
Lane, young Alf opened his coat. He was prepared for
conflict. Round his throat he wore the blue neckerchief,
spotted with white, with which my memory will always
associate him; beneath that a light jersey. His trousers
were supported by a strong leathern belt with a savage-
looking buckle.

Diving into his breast pocket, and glancing cautiously
round, he drew out a handy-looking chopper which he
poised for a moment, as though assuring himself of its
balance.

'That's awright, eh?' he said, putting the chopper in my
hand.

'Are you going to fight with that?' I asked, handing it
back to him.

He passed his hand carefully across the blade.

'That oughter mean forty winks for one or two of 'em.
Don't you fink so?' he said.

His eyes glittered in the light of the gas-lamp as he
thrust the chopper back into his pocket and buttoned up
his coat, having first carefully smoothed down the ends of
his spotted neckerchief.

'Then you'll have a late night, I suppose?' I said as we
passed along up the lane.

"Bout two o'clock I shall be back at my kip,' he replied.

We parted for the night at Vauxhall Cross, where a small crowd of people waited for their trams. We did not shake hands. The ceremony always seems unfamiliar and embarrassing to him. With a curt nod he turned and slid through the crowd, a lithe, well-knit figure, shoulders slightly hunched, turning his head neither to this side nor to that, hands close to his trouser pockets, sneaking his way like a fish through the scattered peril of rocks.

2

Concerning Hooligans

There, was, but a few years ago, a man called Patrick
Hooligan, who walked to and fro among his fellow-men,
robbing them and occasionally bashing them. This much
is certain. His existence in the flesh is a fact as well established as the existence of Buddha or of Mahomet. But with
the life of Patrick Hooligan, as with the lives of Buddha
and of Mahomet, legend has been at work, and probably
many of the exploits associated with his name spring from
the imagination of disciples. It is at least certain that he
was born, that he lived in Irish Court, that he was employed as a chucker-out at various resorts in the neighbourhood. His regular business, as young Alf puts it, was
'giving mugs and other barmy sots the push out of pubs
when their old swank got a bit too thick'. Moreover, he
could do more than his share at tea-leafing, which denotes
the picking up of unconsidered trifles, being handy with
his fingers, and a good man all round. Finally, one day he
had a difference with a constable, put his light out, and
threw the body into a dust-cart. He was lagged, and given
a lifer. But he had not been in gaol long before he had to go
into hospital, where he died.

There is little that is remarkable in this career. But the
man must have had a forceful personality, a picturesque-
ness, a fascination, which elevated him into a type. It was
doubtless the combination of skill and strength, a certain
exuberance of lawlessness, an utter absence of scruple in
his dealings, which marked him out as a leader among men.
Anyhow, though his individuality may be obscured by

14

legend, he lived, and died, and left a great tradition behind him. He established a cult.

The value of a cult is best estimated by its effect upon its adherents, and as Patrick Hooligan is beyond the reach of cross-examination, I propose to devote a few words to showing what manner of men his followers are, the men who call themselves by his name, and do their best to pass the torch of his tradition undimmed to the nippers who are coming on.

I should perhaps not speak of them as men, for the typical Hooligan is a boy who, growing up in the area bounded by the Albert Embankment, the Lambeth Road, the Kennington Road, and the streets about the Oval, takes to tea-leafing as a Grimsby lad takes to the sea. If his taste runs to street-fighting there is hope for him, and for the community. He will probably enlist, and, having helped to push the merits of gin and Christianity in the dark places of the earth, die in the skin of a hero. You may see in Lambeth Walk a good many soldiers who have come back from looking over the edge of the world to see the place they were born in, to smell the fried fish and the second-hand shoe-leather, and to pulsate once more to the throb of a piano-organ. On the other hand, if his fingers be lithe and sensitive, if he have a turn for mechanics, he will slip naturally into the picking of pockets and the rifling of other people's houses.

The home of the Hooligan is, as I have implied, within a stone's throw of Lambeth Walk. Law breakers exist in other quarters of London: Drury Lane will furnish forth a small army of pick-pockets, Soho breeds parasites, and the basher of toffs flourishes in the Kingsland Road. But in and about Lambeth Walk we have a colony, compact and easily handled, of sturdy young villains, who start with a grievance against society, and are determined to get their own back. That is their own phrase, their own view. Life has little to give them but what they take. Honest work, if it can be obtained, will bring in but a few shillings a week; and what is that compared to the glorious possibility of nicking a red 'un?

Small and compact, the colony is easily organized; and here, as in all turbulent communities, such as an English public school, the leader gains his place by sheer force of personality. The boy who has kicked in a door can crow over the boy who has merely smashed a window. If you have knocked-out your adversary at the little boxing place off the Walk, you will have proved that your friendship is desirable. If it becomes known – and it speedily becomes known to all but the police – that you have drugged a toff and run through his pockets, or, better still, have cracked a crib on your own and planted the stuff, then you are at once surrounded by sycophants. Your position is assured, and you have but to pick and choose those that shall work with you. Your leadership will be recognized, and every morning boys, with both eyes skinned for strolling splits, will seek you out and ask for orders for the day. In time, if you stick to work and escape the cops, you may become possessed of a coffee-house or a sweetstuff shop, and run a profitable business as a fence. Moreover, your juniors, knowing your past experience, will purchase your advice – paying for counsel's opinion – when they seek an entrance to a desirable house in the suburbs, and cannot decide between the fanlight and the kitchen window. So you shall live and die respected by all men in Lambeth Walk.

The average Hooligan is not an ignorant, hulking ruffian, beetle-browed and bullet-headed. He is a product of the Board School, writes a fair hand, and is quick at arithmetic. His type of face approaches nearer the rat than the bull-dog; he is nervous, highly-strung, almost neurotic.

He is by no means a drunkard; but a very small quantity of liquor causes him to run amuck, when he is not pleasant to meet. Under-sized as a rule, he is sinewy, swift, and untiring. For pocket-picking and burglary the featherweight is at an advantage. He has usually done a bit of fighting with the gloves, for in Lambeth boxing is one of the most popular forms of sport. But he is better with the raws, and is very bad to tackle in a street row, where there are no rules to observe. Then he will show you some tricks that will astonish you. No scruples of conscience will make him hesitate to butt you in the stomach with his head, and pitch you backwards by catching you round the calves with his arm. His skill, born of constant practice, in scrapping and hurricane fighting brings him an occasional job in the bashing line. You have an enemy, we will say, whom you wish to mark, but, for one reason and another, you do not wish to appear in the matter. Young Alf will take on the job. Indicate to him your enemy; hand him five shillings (he will ask a sovereign; but will take five shillings), and he will make all the necessary arrangements. One night your enemy will find himself lying dazed on the pavement in a quiet corner, with a confused remembrance of a trip and a crash, and a mad whirl of fists and boots. You need have small fear that the job will be bungled. But it is a matter of complaint among the boys of the Walk, that if they do a bit of bashing for a toff and get caught, the toff seldom has the magnanimity to give them a lift when they come out of gaol.

The Hooligan is by no means deficient in courage. He is always ready to fight, though he does not fight fair. It must indeed, require a certain amount of courage to earn your living by taking things that do not belong to you, with the whole of society, backed by the police force, against you. The burglar who breaks into your house and steals your goods is a reprehensible person; but he undoubtedly

possesses that two-o'clock-in-the-morning courage which is
the rarest variety. To get into a stranger's house in the
dead of night, listening every instant for the least sound
that denotes detection, knowing all the time that you are
risking your liberty for the next five years or so – this, I am
sure, requires more nerve than most men can boast of.
Young Alf has nearly all the vices; but he has plenty of
pluck. And as I shall have very little to disclose that is to
his credit, I must tell of one instance in which his conduct
was admirable. One afternoon we were at the Elephant and
Castle, when suddenly a pair of runaway horses, with a
Pickford van behind them, came pounding into the traffic
at the crossing. There was shouting, screaming, and a
scurrying to clear the way, and then I saw young Alf standing alone, tense and waiting, in the middle of the road. It
was a perilous thing to do, but he did it. He was used to
horses, and though they dragged him for twenty yards and
more, he hung on, and brought them up. A sympathetic and
admiring crowd gathered, and young Alf was not a little
embarrassed at the attention he commanded.

'The firm oughter reckernize it,' said a man in an apron,
looking round for approval. 'There's a matter of two
'underd pound's worth of prop'ty that boy's reskid.'

We murmured assent.

'I don't want no fuss,' said young Alf, glancing quickly
around him.

Just then a man ran up, panting and put his hand over
the harness. Then he picked up the reins, and, hoisting
himself by the step, peered into his van.

'You're in luck to-day, mister,' said a boy.

The man passed the back of his hand across a damp
forehead, and sent a dazed look through the crowd.

'One of them blarsted whistles started 'em,' he said.

'That's the boy what stopped 'em,' said a woman with a
basket, pointing a finger at young Alf.

'That's awright,' muttered young Alf. 'You shut yer face.'

'Give the gentleman your name,' persisted the woman with the basket, 'and if everybody 'ad their rights—'

'Now then,' said a friendly policeman, with a hand on young Alf's shoulder, 'you give him your name and address. You want a job, you know. You bin out of work too long.'

Young Alf's brain must have worked very quickly for the next three seconds, and he took the right course. He told the truth. It required an effort. But, as the policeman seemed to know the truth, it would have been silly to tell a lie.

The next day young Alf had the offer of employment, if he would call at headquarters. For a day or two he hesitated. Then he decided that it was not good enough. And that night he went to another kip. By this time he might have been driving a Pickford van. But he never applied for the job.

Regular employment, at a fixed wage, does not attract the boy who is bred within sound of the hawkers in the Walk. It does not give him the necessary margin of leisure, and the necessary margin of chance gains. Many of them hang on to the edge of legitimate commerce as you may see them adhering to the tail-boards of vans; and a van-boy has many opportunities of seeing the world. The selling of newspapers is a favourite occupation. Every Lambeth boy can produce a profession in answer to magisterial interrogation. If you ask young Alf – very suddenly – what his business is, he will reply that he is a horse-plaiter. With time for reflection he may give quite a different answer, according to the circumstances of the case, for he has done many things; watch-making, domestic service, and the care of horses in a travelling circus, have stored his mind with experience and given his fingers deftness.

Young Alf is now eighteen years of age, and stands 5 feet

7 inches. He is light, active, and muscular. Stripped for fighting he is a picture. His ordinary attire consists of a dark-brown suit, mellowed by wear, and a cloth cap. Around his neck is a neatly-knotted neckerchief, dark-blue, with white spots, which does duty for collar as well as tie. His face is by no means brutal; it is intelligent, and gives evidence of a highly-strung nature. The eyes are his most remarkable feature. They seem to look all round his head, like the eyes of a bird; when he is angry they gleam with a fury that is almost demoniacal. He is not prone to smiles or laughter, but he is in no sense melancholic. The solemnity of his face is due rather, as I should conclude, to the concentration of his intellect on the practical problems that continually present themselves for solution. Under the influence of any strong emotions, he puffs out the lower part of his cheeks. This expresses even amusement, if he is very much amused. In his manner of speech he exhibits curious variations. Sometimes he will talk for ten minutes together, with no more trace of accent or slang than disfigure the speech of the ordinary Londoner of the wage-earning class. Then, on a sudden, he will become almost unintelligible to one unfamiliar with the Walk and its ways. He swears infrequently, and drinks scarcely at all. When he does, he lights a fire in the middle of the floor and tries to burn the house down. His health is perfect, and he has never had a day's illness since he had the measles. He has perfect confidence in his own ability to look after himself, and take what he wants, so long as he has elbow-room and ten seconds' start of the cop. His fleetness of foot has earned him the nickname of 'The Deer' in the Walk. On the whole, few boys are better equipped by nature for a life on the crooked, and young Alf has sedulously cultivated his natural gifts.

3
Trailing Clouds of Glory

From heaven young Alf came to Irish Court; but at the
first rumour of his advent, his father went for a soldier,
and so disappears at once and completely from this chronicle. For young Alf never set eyes on his father's chivvy.

His recollections of childhood are, as is natural, scrappy;
here a blank, there a vivid patch of remembrance. But in
the course of various talks he has supplied enough scattered memories to give a fair notion of his earliest outlook
upon life. The flagstones of Irish Court, and the proximity
of Patrick Hooligan, these are the impressions that remain
with him. Cabbage stalks, potato peelings, even derelict
shoes that will no longer go up the spout are to be found on
the flagstones of Irish Court; and with these the untram-
melled infant can do marvellous things. Young Alf cannot remember ever possessing a toy; but he never felt the
want of one. He dealt from infancy in realities.

He retains, too, the impression of a single room, with a
bed in the corner. In another corner was a heap of clothes –
at night. In the day-time, his mother earned her living by
selling second-hand clothes from a hand-barrow in the
Walk. To young Alf, Lambeth Walk was the great world,
full of possibilities of pleasure and profit. Marvellous finds
could be made in the mysterious region under the rows of
barrows in the Walk. Expeditions in search of hidden
treasure were organized, and brought to successful issue,
more particularly in the direction of the sweetstuff barrow,
where brandy-balls might be expected to drop, as it were,
from heaven. There was no lack of companionship, for
children of all ages are plentiful in the Walk, and all are

friends or enemies. Now and then, if he was in luck, he could see Patrick Hooligan come down the court and go into his kip, as a king enters his palace.

On the whole, his childhood must be regarded as a very happy one; his mother was kind to him, and he did pretty much as he pleased, until the School Board officer roped him in, and he had to go to school. Here, of course, he received precisely the same education that five out of six English boys receive. He can read, write a good hand, is thoroughly proficient in mental arithmetic, and retains enough of Biblical learning to quote the parable of the man who fell among thieves.

At twelve years of age he had finished his schooldays. And now his real education was to begin. The problem of life faced him, for round about Lambeth Walk maturity flowers early, and by the time you are twelve years old you must prove your title to existence by fair means or foul. There is little temptation to do it by fair means. This I learned when I met young Alf, one evening in the autumn, in a pleasant room behind the bar of a public-house, which does a genuine trade with the frequenters of the Walk. Strictly speaking, it is not in the Walk. It is quite an ordinary-looking public-house. Anyone may enter. But if you go to the counter, nod to the can – which is the local term for the barman – and make a certain commonplace remark, the can will jerk his head towards a door in the far corner of the bar. This you will push open; and, turning sharp to the right, you will take the second on the left, and find yourself in the pleasant room.

There is really nothing extraordinary about the room. In the midst a table, polished, but showing the stains of glasses; comfortable arm-chairs; on the mantelpiece, spills for such as prefer them; on the table, boxes of matches, two carafes of water, and some sporting-papers; on the walls, advertisements of the 'Canterbury' Music Hall, a sheet containing the portraits of heroes of the prize-ring, photographs of Sir Henry Irving, Miss Marie Lloyd, the late Lord Beaconsfield, and certain ladies who are performing nightly at some place of entertainment in the neighbourhood. Lift the red blind which covers the window and you will look upon a frequented thoroughfare; if you look for more than five minutes, a policeman will walk by and wrinkle his brows at your face. But public feeling inside the room is against the lifting of the blind.

Nor is the company, to outward view, more extraordinary than the room. It consists entirely of men, all of them decently dressed, most of them wearing collars, and some of them in long coats with wonderful buttons, and a way about them that enforces the respect of the can who brings in their drinks. The talk, too, is quite ordinary, playing around the race-course, the drama, and the sex, with a very occasional reference to politics and the police reports. Differing, you will perceive, in no way from the conversation of the average club smoking-room.

There is, however, this difference – that if you should tell a story in which you yourself figured as a successful card-sharper – well, that story would be a great success, supposing you told it well. There is not a man there who would not respect you the more, if he knew you were a burglar in good practice, or a pick-pocket with a large connection; not a man who would not take your part against the police, if you found yourself in a tight corner.

There is, you may think, something melodramatic about that password to the can, the passage behind the bar, the red blind that is not lifted. In reality the whole thing is commonplace – indeed, rather sordid. The point is this: that someone in that assemblage of ordinary men may let fall an indiscreet word which should not be carried into the street, along which a policeman passes at intervals of a few minutes, and a split at intervals which are irregular.

This was the room to which I found my way one evening in the autumn, guided by the admonitions of young Alf. He was awaiting me. Otherwise the room was untenanted, save by a man with a grey beard, who sipped his glass in a corner. And it was here that I caught some of those flashes of memory which I try to reflect.

We were seated, more or less comfortably. For young Alf does not sit easily in an easy-chair, but leans forward, alert and ready to run, dodge, dive and come safely to his desired kip.

'No, I didn't go to no reg'lar work when I'd done my schooling,' said young Alf. 'You see, I was well in the thick of where the lads carry on the biz; nor I didn't see no great catch in any sort of job that I was likely to get 'old of. It come much more easy and natural to take on the light-fingered game, an' there was more to be made at it. See? An' when I'd got meself mixed up wiv the young part of the gang, it wasn't much good me goin' lookin' for work wiv a crac'ter that wasn't long enough to light a pipe wiv. Sims to me what you start on you've got to go froo wiv. First fing ever I nicked was pigeons – an' rabbits. Down Irish Court stewed pigeons an' rabbits is a bit of awright. There wasn't anyfink that my muvver liked better. Dogs, too—'

'But you didn't eat dogs?' I said.

'No, we didn't eat 'em. But if you can pick up a stray dog, there's generally a bit of a reward 'anging to it.'

I suggested that there were scarcely enough stray dogs about to bring in an appreciable income.

'Oh, they'll stray awright,' said young Alf, 'even if you 'ave to pull their bleed'n 'eads 'arf off.'

It was at about this period of his life that young Alf removed from Irish Court and took up his residence over a shop – to all appearances belonging to a watchmaker – in one of the streets that cut Lambeth Walk; and here his education began to move rapidly forward.

'Me an' my muvver,' he said, 'was livin' wiv a clown an' accerabat that used to give performances in some of the smaller 'alls round abart. He was a fair treat, that accerabat was. Stand on his 'ead, an' tie 'isself up in knots until you'd fink he crack 'isself. He could bend right back till you could see his dial stickin' out 'tween his legs. There wasn't 'ardly anyfink he couldn't do, not in that way. Bit of a 'ook, too, 'e was.

'Well, one evenin' 'e was sittin' on the bed, mendin' his shoes, an' I was over by the windy. Presently 'e says to me: "Look 'ere, young Alf, you see if you can walk across to me quiet as you can."

'So I started, walkin' as quiet as I knew how, but I couldn't 'elp makin' the floor creak, 'cause the board was all loose.

'The accerabat jumps up and catches me a clip over the jaw.

' "Now then," 'e says, "you start again. An' every time you make a board creak, I'll clip yer." See?

'I went on practisin' that game for some time, and the accerabat showed me 'ow to nip across a floor wivout making a sound. An' it wasn't long, neither, 'fore I could step so as you couldn't 'ear nuffink. That's the first fing you have to learn, an' it ain't so bloomin' easy, neither. Taught me a lot of fings, the accerabat did. There was a old tin trunk standin' over side of the bed; and when I'd learnt to get across the floor awright, 'e took me on to openin' the tin trunk wivout makin' any noise. That's abart the most difficult job you 'ave to work – if you're in a strange 'ouse, I mean, and don't want to wake anybody up. If you can open a tin trunk quite quiet you can do almost anyfink in that line.'

'Did the acrobat go in for burglary, then?' I asked, as young Alf relapsed into a meditative silence.

Presently he looked up, and puffed out the lower portion

of his cheeks three times, thereby indicating an amusing recollection.

'What'd you fink of me in a Eton suit, an' a black bowler 'at, and a nice white collar when I was a nipper, eh?'

The picture seemed an interesting one, and I said as much.

'One night I was messin' about in the Walk,' said young Alf, 'and my muvver comes along and catches me by the frottle, an' says, "You come along 'ome; you're wanted." So I went along wiv 'er, an' when we got to our kip there was the accerabat an' anuvver bloke, a pal of his, what I hadn't seen afore. The uvver bloke 'ad a black bag wiv 'im, and, soon as he sees me, he opens the bag an' brings out a nice suit of clothes. "You jest get into them togs," says the accerabat, "and look slippy about it." Course I tumbled at once that there was a bit of work on 'and, and I got into the togs wivout arstin' any questions. Reg'lar little toff I looked, wiv me clean collar and me black jacket, and me grey trowsies.' Young Alf leaned back in his chair, grasped the arms with dingy fingers, and puffed his pallid cheeks in joy at the recollection.

'Well, when I'd got me togs on,' continued young Alf, 'out we goes, me an' the accerabat an' 'is pal, me walkin' behind and carryin' the little bag, an' the uvver two in front. Course if anyone wanted to know anyfink, I was to swank as I hadn't got anyfink to do wiv the uvver two. See?

'Time we got down to Kennington Park Road it was gettin' pretty late, wiv scarcely any people about. The accerabat an' his pal stopped outside a big boot-shop, an' the accerabat took my little bag, and, the uvver bloke says, "Now then, young 'un, up you goes." An' wiv that he give me a shove up, and 'fore you could turn round I was froo the fanlight and down on the uvver side. Course I was quiet as a mouse, an' when I found nobody'd 'eard any-fink, I jest sat down and waited till the uvver bloke outside give me the wheeze he was ready. See?'

'Then, how did you know what to do?' I asked.

'Anybody'd know that,' replied young Alf. 'Soon as I 'eard the whistle outside, I goes over the bolts – free bolts there was – and turns the key, an' lets in the accerabat an' 'is pal. The uvver bloke 'ands me my bag, an' there was me walkin' carm and peaceful back to me kip in me nice Eton suit, an' me black bowler, an' me grey trowsies, carryin' the little bag in me 'and.'

'But why the little bag?' I asked.

'Didn't I tell you?' said young Alf; 'there was a surplus in the little bag.'

'A—'

'What you wear in church. So, if a cop wanted to know what I was after I'd say I was a choir-boy bin practisin' carols. Then 'e'd open my little bag an' find a surplus there. An' that'd bear me out. See? It was the accerabat's pal what gives me the togs an' the surplus. Smart 'e was – very smart – in a small way, but no class. Arrever, I did my little bit of biz that time awright.'

Young Alf crossed his legs and sat back in his chair, with the air of a young man who has at least one memory which he can contemplate with satisfaction. He would have a small ginger-beer – nothing stronger – and a cigar. And thus stimulated, he dug again into the past, and told me more concerning the days when he was scrapping in the Walk, nicking pigeons for his mother's supper, and jumping fanlights for the barren glory of wearing an Eton suit from ten o'clock to midnight or thereabouts. Occupations creditable enough to a boy of twelve, but certainly not class, and to be referred to only as Lord Tenterden referred to the barber's shop.

The watchmaker in the shop below the room in which

young Alf kipped with his mother and the acrobat was, as
you will have guessed, not an ordinary watchmaker. In his
leisure hours young Alf would hang about the shop, with
an eye on the labours of his landlord. Having a turn for
mechanics, and possessing a pair of hooks that were lithe
and sensitive, he amused himself by performing some of the
simpler operations connected with the repairing of watches,
and soon picked up a certain acquaintance with the craft.
Before long he noticed that the watchmaker had a sur-
prising number of watches to repair. It struck him too that
each watch-owner appeared to be dissatisfied with the
case enclosing his ticker, for his landlord always began his
task by transferring the works from one gold case to
another. From this young Alf drew his inferences. He concluded that those watches were not the lawful property of
the sellers, nor of the watchmaker, who gave a ridiculously
small price for them. In short, he decided that his landlord
was a fence; and subsequent happenings confirmed his
judgement. And one day young Alf slipped half-a-dozen
gold watch-cases into his jacket pocket. Of course they
were missed. But as young Alf had foreseen, the watchmaker dared not place the matter in the hands of the police,
though he made no secret of the direction of his suspicions.
Moreover, young Alf, finding a certain difficulty in the
disposal of his goods, finally brought them boldly to his
landlord and demanded a price for them. He obtained it,
on the understanding that if he should pick up any more
articles of value in a similarly accidental way his landlord
should have the refusal of their purchase. Thus young Alf
established his first confidential relations with a fence.

But young Alf was anxious to gain some official recognition. At present he was technically only a fanlight-
jumper, who gave promise of being handy with his hooks
in the way of nicking and scrapping. That does not satisfy
the ambition of a boy who is within sight of his thirteenth

birthday. Such a boy, with the proper spirit in him, wants
to get into a gang. For this merit is the sole qualification.

'Course I wanted to get into a gang,' said young Alf,
swallowing half a bottle of ginger-beer at a gulp. He never
sips, but throws, as it were, his drink down his throat.
'But you can't get into a gang wivout you've done somefink big. It's like this. See? S'pose one boy goes an' kicks in
a door. Then he tells the uvver boys, and shows 'em the
door. Then they got to go an' kick in anuvver door, else
they're no class. An' course the boy what done somefink
big, what the uvver boys couldn't follow up – well, 'e's
class. See? An' 'cept you've done somefink class, you can't
get took into a gang. I told you about the accerabat that
me an' my muvver was livin' wiv? Well, there was a
Institute down off the Old Kent Road, where there was a
entertainment one night – sort of 'sault-of-arms mostly,
an' the accerabat was givin' a performance there. So 'e
says, "Come along wiv me and look after the props."
So course I went, an' got behind the stage. Well, there was
a lot of gents takin' part, an' they'd took off their togs and
'ung 'em all round the dressing-room. Now's my time, I
finks. An' soon as the accerabat'd got into 'is props, an'
was on the stage for his performance, I slips froo to the
dressing-room and goes froo all the pockets what I could
finger. What wiv one fing an' anuvver, I managed to nick
a matter of ten pounds or so. Then I nipped off and planted
the stuff where it couldn't come to no 'arm, and couldn't
'urt nobody, an' 'fore the second part of the performance
was started, there was me, 'anging about premiskus at the
back of the 'all. I got back jest in time to hear the chairman
give out that there was thieves about, an' advisin' the
audience to look after their pockets. When the gents had
gone to take off their athaletic dress, they'd found that
someone 'ad been looking after their prop'ty more careful
than what they had. Course I wasn't suspected, me 'anging

about all the time where everybody could see me. See? An'
wivout a penny in me pocket. See?

'So when the performance was over, an' we were goin'
along to our kip, I told the accerabat 'ow I'd done a bit of
biz on me own, 'cause I couldn't keep it to meself. An' 'e
says: "Got the stuff on yer, ye young devil?" 'e says. "What
d' you fink?" I says. "I planted it." Then the accerabat
wanted to know where I'd planted it, an' I says it's likely
I'd tell him, bein' me own stuff. See? An' wiv that he was
comin' for me frottle; but I ducked under 'is arm an'
scooted, nor I didn't go 'ome that night, nor yet for two
nights arter. Two days I laid low, and then I went an'
lifted the stuff where I'd planted it. Finks 'e was goin' to
'andle the stuff that b'longed to me. Likely!' Young Alf
shot the remainder of the ginger-beer down his throat.

'Not 'im,' he said, as he put down his glass, and threw
back his head, taking a long whiff of his cigar.

'Actors is pretty fly gen'rally,' he continued presently,
'but they get made a mark of now an' then, 'specially when
they're new to the biz. You show 'em the way to the stage
door. See? It's always in a dark alley or a side street wiv
no light. Then you walk right in; don't 'ang about; an'
everybody'll fink you belong to the place. An' if you keep
your eyes skinned, the place'll belong to you. Won't take
you free minutes nor more to run froo the dressing-rooms.
Why, you can 'urry past the bloke at the door jest as if you
was late for your performance, and get froo all alone.
There's lots of women prigs that works that line, goin' froo
the rooms where the lady artists change. An' they can
make a tidy bit out of it, wiv no error.'

Young Alf puffed even more vigorously at his cigar.

But dishonest endeavour is never utterly wasted, and
the exploit at the School of Arms, admirably executed as it
was, proved to be a turning-point in young Alf's career.
The incident should be a lesson to young men starting in

life, that the smallest opportunity is too good to be neglected, and that the decision of a moment may lead to an assured position among their fellows.

For, as appears from young Alf's narrative, the rumour ran round the Walk that young Alf had done something class on his own, and, as you may well believe, young Alf was not inclined to minimize his merits. One boy whispered to another, and in no long time this ten pounds was multiplied by ten. Probably there were sceptics who doubted young Alf's capacity; others, too, who thought that so young a nipper should not be thrust into premature prominence. But when young Alf, having lifted his stuff and invested it carefully, appeared in the Walk with a brown coat, and the usual trimmings of buttons, a bowler hat, and a pair of trousers cut very saucy, well, there was nothing more to be said.

Young Alf was, in a sense, class. He had proved himself a boy of enterprise, able to conceive and execute a successful plan; a boy, too, who knew how to spend money as well as how to acquire it. For he and the other boys went on the razzle down the Walk, and his ten pounds was beginning to look very small indeed. Nevertheless, it was no longer necessary to kick in doors in order to earn respect.

You never know what the smallest job, well executed, may prelude. This little exploit, which to young Alf's mature judgement is scarcely worth consideration, was one of the turning-points of his career, and led to what we may call his first regular employment.

For some time young Alf had been aware of the eye of Billy the Snide upon him; and it was no small thing to attract the attention of Billy the Snide, who was in a big line and able to give a lift to an older hand than young Alf. Once or twice Billy the Snide had gone out of his way to kick young Alf off the pavement in the Walk, which encouraged young Alf to hope for better things. His exploit was by this time getting talked about; for no one had the least doubt as to the fate of that missing money, except the police, who are sticklers for evidence.

It was in the Kennington Road that Billy the Snide stepped into young Alf's life, and gave him the promotion he had earned.

One afternoon he was walking down the Kennington Road, clad in his new coat; in his mouth a cigar. For he had still nearly a sovereign left from his haul at the School of Arms, and could afford his little comforts. He was much pleased with himself, for he had just bought a new cap which had taken his fancy, and bought it cheap. It had lain in the shilling heap outside the shop, but a shilling seemed an excessive price when sixpence was enough. So he had shifted it from the shilling basket to the sixpenny basket while making his selection, and sprung a tanner. He looks back with a certain pride on the transaction, for it was the last occasion on which he found it necessary to pay cash for an article of dress.

He was in excellent spirits as he walked the Kennington Road, clad in his new overcoat and newer cap, and encountered Billy the Snide.

Now, Billy the Snide was a leader of men, and looked up to by such as young Alf.

He has described to me the meeting more than once, conscious that it marked a crisis in his life.

The interview was short, the details are few and simple, but pregnant with fate.

Billy the Snide did not kick young Alf off the pavement, as was his custom, and that in itself was significant.

''Old on,' said Billy, as young Alf was about to pass him respectfully.

Young Alf halted.

It was as though the Lord Chancellor should stop a rising

junior in the Strand, and ask him if he had a moment to spare.

'Bit slippy wiv yer 'ooks, I'm given to unnerstand,' remarked Billy the Snide, looking critically over young Alf.

'They're me own 'ooks, so far's I'm told,' retorted young Alf, almost blushing at the compliment. 'Feel like it.'

Billy the Snide spat reflectively at a passing hansom, and, satisfied that he had hit the mark, turned again to young Alf.

'Like to work 'long 'er me?' said Billy the Snide, being a man of few words, and those words to the point.

Like to work along of him! Who wouldn't? Would a briefless barrister like to devil for an Attorney-General? Who wouldn't chuck fanlight-jumping, and pigeon-nicking, and aimless scrapping in the side streets off the Walk, in order to work with Billy the Snide.

Young Alf's cigar was extinguished in his joy, but Billy the Snide gave him another; and that evening he walked home to his kip through the stars.

Billy the Snide has come to grief since then, and now his number is up. But he gave young Alf a good start, and when all is said and done they had a stirring week together, of which he promised to tell me on the following evening.

4
Billy the Snide

So young Alf took service with Billy the Snide, and felt that
he had his foot well on the first rung of the ladder whereby
a boy may mount to an honoured old age as a publican or a
fence.

On the evening after the conversation recounted in the
previous chapter I pushed open the swing-door of the
public-house off the Walk, and found young Alf engaged in
conversation with the can. He nodded to me, and led the
way through the door at the far end of the bar. As I
reached the door, I caught the eye of the can.

'Same line?' he said, jerking his head towards the door
through which young Alf had disappeared.

'Just at present,' I replied.

I was not quite certain for the moment as to his meaning,
but I think I told the truth. For the present young Alf and
I were a pair of literary men.

We had the pleasant room to ourselves, for we were
rather early, and there was a race-meeting somewhere in
the neighbourhood of London, and the boys had not yet
returned to town.

'I been finkin'!' said young Alf, rubbing his close-
cropped head with a grimy hand. 'I said I'd tell you 'ow we
worked the biz, me an' Billy, an' I fink I can remember
most about it.'

'What was his real name?' I asked.

He hesitated for a few moments.

'Bill Day was 'is name,' he said presently. 'But we
never called 'im nuffink but Billy, or Billy the Snide.
Everybody'd know who you meant. If you'd sent a tally-

gram to 'im by that name, 'e'd a' got it. But you couldn't tallygraft to Billy no more. His number's up awright, wiv no error.'

Bill, as I have implied, has pegged out, a victim to sundry disorders mostly of his own creating. I inquired of his appearance in the flesh, but young Alf, though frequently graphic in the delineation of events, is not an adept at describing personalities. It was only by careful cross-examination that I gained any idea of Billy the Snide's outward aspect, and my idea may differ entirely from the photograph which has been buried somewhere in Scotland Yard. I have the impression of a man above the middle height, clean shaven, of stern and perhaps forbidding exterior; a man who limped slightly in one foot, owing to a sudden leap from a first-floor window on to the area railings; a man observant, but reticent; a man who said nothing but what he meant to be believed; a man who always wore a bowler hat. Such is the impression of Billy the Snide that I have brought away. It is too meagre. I regret exceedingly that I never saw him before he snuffed out, for he was a leader of men, and his memory is still green in the Walk, where there is nothing green but is plucked.

Billy the Snide was in a pretty big way of business; he did not, you will understand, depend on his day's takings for the price of his kip. He was the owner of a pony and a barrow, as well as of a missus. He managed to feed and clothe himself, as well as certain people who had a more or less illegal claim upon him on the margin of profit left by counterfeit half-crowns, enjoying, too, ample intervals of leisure. Karl Alley was his address. Karl Alley cheek-by-jowl with Irish Court, runs off China Walk, and is a nasty corner for a green hand to find himself in after dark. Here Billy the Snide had a room; and by means of a few simple appliances he imitated the products of the Mint. But snide coin takes a bit of passing, and Billy was glad of the help of a smart youngster, who had done something class in the way of nicking to show he was up to the work; a youngster, too, whose appearance disarmed suspicion, for young Alf tells me that, in those days his face was almost saintly in its purity, more especially when he was permitted to wear an Eton suit. We may suspect that a touch of worldliness was added to his aspect when he wore his new overcoat and his new cap, and was smoking a cigar.

Henceforth, for a few days of crowded life, it was the office of young Alf to throw bad money after good. He still lived with his mother and the acrobat, but every morning he went round to Karl Alley to arrange the work for the day; and there was a lot of jealousy among the boys who had never got beyond tea-leafing, which is creditable, but not class. He looks back upon this period of his life with considerable pride, for promotion went by merit alone in the circle of which Billy the Snide was the centre, and no boy would have been taken on to work with him unless he had given evidence of capacity. Young Alf was not yet thirteen, and very young to occupy so responsible a position of trust.

So young Alf was a proud boy when he turned into Karl Alley on the first morning of his engagement, and sought out the dwelling of his chief.

In order to try his hand and acquire confidence, young Alf was sent out on a small job alone. Billy the Snide produced a wrong 'un, and bade young Alf plant it at a big house near the Walk – the house to which you take mugs who have been marked for skinning.

Young Alf set forth, while Billy the Snide awaited the result in Karl Alley. It was nervous work, for young Alf was aware that they knew a bit at that house; moreover, he felt that his future depended on his present success. He waited a bit outside until he saw through the swing-doors that the can was busy. Then he entered, gave his order, planked his bull's-eye on the counter, and came out with four and elevenpence change.

Billy the Snide expressed approval, gave young Alf a shilling for himself, and for the next day proposed an expedition on a far more sumptuous scale.

The next morning they started, a pleasant family party, from the Walk, in Billy the Snide's pony-barrow; Billy and the missus in front, and young Alf sitting on the empty baskets at the tail-board. You would have said, had you met them trotting along the Brixton Road, that they were going to market. Indeed, Billy the Snide was wont to describe himself, when publicly invited to declare his occupation, as a general dealer.

Round Brixton, Stockwell, and Clapham they drove on a career of uninterrupted prosperity, pulling up at public-houses, and now and then at a likely looking small shop. The best kind of small shop is one which is looked after by a woman whose husband is working elsewhere. Meanwhile Billy's right-side trouser pocket was growing rapidly lighter, and the left one, containing honest metal, was pleasantly heavy. Young Alf, too, had half-a-sovereign as his own share in his waistcoat pocket.

It was past noon when they reached Wandsworth Common, and Billy the Snide pulled up the pony at a house he had decided to work. Young Alf and the missus entered together, while Billy the Snide remained without by the pony-barrow so as to be ready in case of a scoot.

'What are you takin', missus?' asked young Alf.

The missus said that her call was for the usual – half-a-quartern of gin and two out. Young Alf slashed down a bull's-eye for the drink, and the can, being suspicious, picked it up and put his lamps over it. Young Alf, being about to gargle, set down his glass.

'Missus, we're rumbled,' he said.

For the can had walked up to the bung with the coin, and the bung was walking with the coin to the tester. The tester was consulted, and for answer split the bull's-eye into halves.

The bung slid up to young Alf and the missus.

'That's a bad 'un,' said the bung, holding out the two halves of the detected coin. 'D'you know that?'

'Bad!' exclaimed young Alf.

'Good Gawd! To think of that!' said the missus, looking struck all of a heap.

'Well, guv'nor,' said young Alf, 'I'm in for a bit of a loss out of my 'ard week's graft froo that coin gettin' in wiv the uvvers; an' if I've got any more I shall look what ho!'

Young Alf pulled from his waistcoat pocket the half thick 'un which was his share of the profits.

'D'you mind puttin' one of these in the fake?' said young Alf.

The coin was put through the tester and came out intact. Whereupon the bung reckoned it was a shame that young Alf should have been taken in with the five-shilling piece.

'It's very kind of you to symperfise wiv us, boss,' said young Alf, finishing his ginger-beer.

'Now you 'ave one with me,' said the bung, looking at the empty glasses.

The missus said she would have another of the same. But young Alf, noting the sudden absence of the can, concluded that he had gone for a cop. It was clear that the bung was having some of his old swank.

'Step short, missus,' said young Alf. And wishing the bung 'good-afternoon', they scooted.

'It didn't take us 'arf a mo to shift soon as joinin' Billy,' said young Alf in concluding his narrative of the day's adventures. 'An' sharper'n any cop ever put down 'is daisy roots, we was round the corner an' out of sight.'

Altogether it was a day of pleasure and of profit.

To this succeeded three days of joy and gain; days on which young Alf viewed the world as it stretched southward to Denmark Hill, and eastward to the 'Bricklayer's Arms', sitting proudly upon the empty baskets at the tail of Billy the Snide's pony-barrow. Impartially and conscientiously they worked South London; and young Alf's share of the swag ran into something like fifteen shillings a day, on the average. Young Alf confesses that these were among the happiest days of his life, for fresh air is good, and driving is good, and fifteen shillings a day is very good indeed, so long as it lasts; much better than three-and-six a week as an honest errand-boy.

'I don't ever fink I made more'n that since, not day in, day out,' said young Alf, as he told me the story of the six days.

But success made them reckless. The fifth day was the last of triumph. It was down Battersea way that the last victory was scored, a victory that led to defeat. I would not spoil young Alf's artless story; it must be given in his own words, as he told it to me in that pleasant room behind the bar of the public-house off Lambeth Walk. He told it, sitting well forward in his chair, with quick glances this way and that way, and with no turn of the head all the time, his hands between his knees, and his cap bunched in his hands.

'Gettin' well down into Battersea,' said young Alf, 'Billy marked a small shop where there was a ole woman be'ind the counter. So he give me the wheeze, an' says, "You slip in there, cocker." An' presently he pulls up the pony, and I nips back an' goes into the shop. The ole woman was stannin' be'ind the counter.

' "'Arf-a-dozen eggs, missus, an' new laid," I says. "We always keep 'em fresh," says the ole woman. "Well, I want 'em for someone that's snuffin' it," I told 'er. "Wort you

39

mean?" she chipped in, not 'ankin'. "Well, peggin' out,"
I eggsplained. So she says, "Dyin', I s'pose you mean," an'
'andin' me the wobblers. Down I planks a two-hog piece,
an' she picked it up an' fair screamed. "That's bad," she
calls out. "I've 'ad one like it afore to-day," she says – the
old geezer. "Bad, missus!" I says. "I'd like to 'ave a cart-
load of 'em."

'She didn't say nuffink to that, but she turned round and
called out to somebody in the parlour be'ind the shop, an'
out comes a bloke wiv a razzo like 'arf a boiled beetroot, or
I don't know nuffink about it. Looked as if you wouldn't
like to pay for the 'arf of what 'e could lower. Well, ole
ruby boko put 'is lamps over me, wiv no error, an' he says,
"Why you're the youngster as come in 'ere afore." An' wiv
that he picks up the snide. Then I chips in. "Well," I says,
"then you can testerfy to my respecterability." 'Cause,
you unnerstand, I 'adn't never bin wivin 'arf-a-mile of the
shop in me life. "The money's bad," he goes on, runnin' it
'tween 'is fingers.

'So then I made out as if I was cross, and I says, "What
the bleedin' 'ell d'you mean?" I says. "If you finks I've
cheated you, or if you finks I've tried to cheat you, then
send for the p'lice," I says. Course I see my game, 'cause
old ruby boko was 'tween me an' the door. See?'

Young Alf shot a cunning glance at me; and, after a
moment's reflection, I saw.

Young Alf leaned well forward in his chair and puffed
out his cheeks, whence I inferred an amusing reminiscence. Then he continued his story.

'Wiv that out 'e goes, an' pulls the door of the shop
be'ind 'im, so's to cage me while 'e fetches the cops; an'
that's a pretty long job, as a general rule. Course that was
just what I wanted. In 'arf a mo I was over the counter an'
slashin' at the ole woman. Caught 'er one under the chib,
an' she give a scream, an' dropped on to the floor like a wet

40

sack. There wasn't no one else in the 'ouse, so I got to work quick, and went froo the till. It wasn't much of a 'aul – nuffink to talk about. I don't fink there was more'n free twoers worf to be nicked. But it was worf more'n bein' pinched, eh? Well, I was out of the shop in a tick, an' there was Billy an' the missus on the pony-barrer, carm and peaceful, jest up by the corner where the road turns off. Course I give Billy the wheeze quick as I could, an' 'e whips up the pony jest as I 'opped up be'ind. An' jest as we drove off there was old ruby boko about a 'undred yards away, running as fast as the cop could keep time to wiv 'is plates o' meat. See?'

But as I have already said, this was the last day of triumph for Billy the Snide, who was pretty well at the end of his tether. There are some things that even the police force cannot overlook, and the doings of Billy were crying to Heaven. Over-production, it seems, was the bane of Billy the Snide. Not content with doing a moderate and comparatively safe retail trade, Billy had made haste to be rich, and had placed a nice little lot of snide money with a pal. There was bad management somewhere, for the pal had been putting it about over the same ground which Billy and young Alf were covering; and the splits were on the look-out.

It was on the following day that the catastrophe came about.

'Never you carry snide coin on your person, 'cept when you want to put it about,' said young Alf, as he told me the story of Billy's downfall. 'An' if you fink you've incurred suspicion, you frow it all away quick as you can. Never mind 'ow much it is. Frow it away. You can 'ford that more'n you can 'ford doing a stretch. An' if they don't find nuffink on your person, why, they can't do nuffink to you. See? You can say it was a mistake, you 'avin' a snide coin at all. See?'

Disregard of this advice, which had been given to him by Billy the Snide, nearly cost young Alf his liberty on that fatal morning. He was coming round as usual to Billy's residence to organize the day's graft, flushed with the pride of success, and carrying in his pocket a quantity of base metal which would have represented about the value of a sovereign had it been honest money. As he was about to turn into Karl Alley he was suddenly aware of a split hanging about. To give Billy the wheeze was to give himself away. Young Alf had decided to go home again and wait upon events, when he found himself rushed before he could turn round. A copper took him off to the police station.

The situation looked desperate, for a pound's worth of snide coin is difficult to explain away; and young Alf felt pretty certain that the game was up.

But his luck did not desert him. When they reached the police station the inspector happened to have stepped out for a few moments, so young Alf was dabbed into a cell to await his return.

This was his opportunity, and he did not neglect it. No sooner was the door closed than he cleared the snide coin out of his pockets, and pitched it into the most obvious receptacle.

'I knew it was awright then,' said young Alf. 'I jest 'ad time to go froo a bit of a double-shuffle step on the floor of the cell – showin' I wasn't disturbed in me mind, you unnerstand – and then the cop came to take me before the inspector, an' run me froo to see what I 'ad on my person. That's what they say in evidence, y'know.

'Course they didn't find any snide coin on me person, an' as I 'adn't anyfink in the way of good money, it was a case of bein' clean picked. I never see a copper look so seprised in all me born days; looked as if you might 'ave brought 'im down wiv 'arf a brick. The inspector 'e was jest knocked sick, 'e was. Fort they'd got me proper that time, they did. But I reckon if I 'aven't got any sharpness of me own, I got 'old of a little bit of someone else's that time, eh?'

I replied that the incident did him infinite credit.

Young Alf pinched the end of his cigar, and put the stump into his waistcoat pocket.

'So you got off?' I said.

'The inspector told me I could 'ook it,' said young Alf. 'But d'you fink I was going like that? Not me. Not wivout giving 'em somefink thick in the way of slanging. "What d'yer mean?" I says. "What d'yer mean by interferin' wiv a 'ard-working boy in the performance of 'is employment? I can tell you," I says, "I got my livin' to look after; and now I lost me morning's work jest because a silly swine of a cop don't know a honest boy from a thief. An' I can tell you straight," I says, "I don't get rabbit-pie fair chucked at me, neither." '

That was enough. They bundled him out of the police station by main force. For if you want to make a copper very angry indeed, you have only to mention to him the name of rabbit-pie. It has the same effect on a policeman as an allusion to puppy-pie has on a Thames bargeman. This is one of the many things that young Alf knows.

I inquired the reason of this strange aversion.

'Gives a cop the indigestion,' explained young Alf,' even if you only talk to 'im about it. But I don't believe anyone that know'd a p'liceman personally would ever think of foolin' 'im wiv such a snack. Rabbit-pie might do for fillin' up odd corners, but if you 'arst 'im to make a banquet off it, why, 'e wouldn't be takin' any.'

I think there must be some better explanation than that.

But Karl Alley knew Billy the Snide no more. The cops rushed him while young Alf was being run through at the police station.

'Billy the Snide an' 'is missus bofe fell,' said young Alf,

as he recounted the melancholy story; 'an' for a week or two it was a case of looking round and about for your 'umble. But I laid low, an' the pair of 'em, 'avin been before the beak twice on remand froo me bein' wanted to make the party complete, they was sent for trial.'

It was a terrible set-back for young Alf, who was just beginning to get on; the more especially as Billy had taught him only how to pass snide coin, and not how to make it.

Young Alf had pitched away his stock of base money, and had very little of the ordinary kind. Nevertheless, he kept a brave heart, knowing that a boy who had worked with Billy the Snide could not long be out of employment. Meanwhile, he sold newspapers outside Waterloo Station, and kept his eyes skinned for chances.

In the evening papers he read how Billy and the missus came up for trial; how Billy was given an eight years' stretch, while the missus had a twelvemonth that she could call her own, and no one else's; how Billy, undaunted by his fate, made the approved retort – that he could do that little lot on his napper, and was thereafter removed from the sight of men.

Billy the Snide has, as I have said, snuffed out. But he was a good 'un in his time. He gave young Alf his start, taught him many useful wheezes, and was not ungenerous in the division of swag; and young Alf always speaks very nicely about him.

5
Jimmy

We were sitting together on the Embankment, and talked, to the accompaniment of the rumble of trains over the bridge at Charing Cross. It was a warm evening for the season of the year; and young Alf preferred an outdoor conversation, because he wished to keep his napper cool. Later on he had, as it appeared, an appointment in the neighbourhood of Regent's Park, the nature of which he did not disclose, nor did I inquire.

Once or twice as we talked a policeman paced slowly past us, and turned a flash of his lantern on to the seat. But young Alf is by no means nervous in face of a constable in uniform. If you have a difference of opinion with a policeman your course is extremely simple. Your object is to get past him. Do not dodge, do not hesitate.

'You put yer 'ed down and run at 'is belly,' is young Alf's simple prescription. 'Then you walk down the next to the left. That's the sawftest place about a cop, wiv no error. Run! Wot yer talkin' abart?'

Young Alf spat contemptuously.

In the Walk young Alf is sometimes spoken of familiarly as 'The Deer', and he prides himself on meriting the nickname.

Having half-an-hour to spare before leaving for his engagement in North London, young Alf dwelt upon the interval in his life during which he was bereft of Billy the Snide and had not yet found favour in the eyes of Jimmy. It was a lean month, during which he sold newspapers and kept an eye skinned for an opening. The month was chiefly memorable on account of a purse he nicked in the neighbourhood of Waterloo Station. There was a fog about at the time, and the woman had lost her way. Young Alf has the good feeling to admit his debt to the teaching of the acrobat. But it was a simple, straightforward job, and scarcely worth mention, except as his first essay in highway robbery. Also the success gave him confidence.

Of course young Alf knew Jimmy by sight as well as by repute, though it was rather too much to hope that Jimmy took more than a casual interest in him. But one night Jimmy bought an evening paper from young Alf, gave him a penny, and did not press for the change. Jimmy regarded young Alf for a moment or two, then he said:

'What you sellin' papers for? 'Bout time you was doin' better'n that.'

'Best fing I can fink of,' replied young Alf, and Jimmy walked on, disappointing young Alf.

Now Jimmy – who had enough surnames to fill a birth-day-book – occupied an assured position as a burglar with a large visiting list. But Jimmy was waxing fat with prosperity, and growing a little too stout for the active work of his profession. The stairs bothered him – for of course you have to ascend by the banisters for fear of electric bells and suchlike modern fakements. It was therefore natural that Jimmy should be shifting the rough work on to the younger generation and taking matters a bit easy himself.

Jimmy, in fact, had a gang under him, and since the pinching of Pat Hooligan had been the recognized leader of the Lambeth boys who worked on the crooked.

Young Alf had lost his boss; and though he had gained in reputation from working with Billy the Snide, he had no inkling of the good fortune that was to fall to him.

It came one evening in Paradise Street.

'I'd had a bit of a argyment,' said young Alf, 'wiv

anuvver boy that was sellin' papers like me outside
Waterloo Station. An' comin' down the Walk later on I
met him accidental, an' 'e says, "Garn, young Alf, you're
'fraid." An' I said he was a bleed'n' liar. An' in 'arf a mo we
was up Paradise Street, an' scrappin' all we know'd. I
should 'a' beat 'im easy, beat 'is 'ed off. Only 'fore I could
get at 'im proper I felt myself pulled off by the collar of me
coat, an' there was Jimmy luggin' me round the corner.
Soon as we got out of sight of the uvvers Jimmy let go of
me an' says, "Let me p'int out to you," 'e says, "that
scrappin' in the 'ighways an' 'edges ain't no class at all."
Jimmy was always one for talk, 'e was. "What do you
want to go an' make yourself conspickyus for?" says
Jimmy. Then Jimmy goes on to say 'ow he knowed of a
bit o' stuff I could put me 'ooks on if I was game. Course I
answers back that I was game enough. What do you fink?

' "Fact is," says Jimmy, "there's a 'ouse that I've 'ad
waxed for about a week down Denmark Hill way. It's a
easy job," says Jimmy, "but if you like to come alonger
me and lend a 'and it'll be comp'ny like. See?" "I'm wiv
you," I says. "Well," says Jimmy, "you come 'an 'ave a
snack at a cawfy-'ouse, and then you wait a bit while I
goes and fetches the tools. It'll be about time to start
then." '

Young Alf went and had his snack with Jimmy, and
then sat and waited in great contentment while Jimmy
went for the tools.

He was of course very happy, for to be noticed at all by
such a man as Jimmy was a privilege; to work with him
was glory. A little nervous, too, because this was the first
job of the kind in which he had taken part – putting aside
fanlight jumping, which really does not count – but very
happy. Moreover, Jimmy was known to be a very safe
man to work with. He had a way of eluding the police, and
never spared pains in taking all reasonable precautions

beforehand. In fact, Jimmy at this period could boast of never having been arrested for years. And to this day he walks – with some difficulty, due to increasing bulk – a free man among his fellow-men.

6

Class!

The rest of the story of that momentous evening young
Alf told me as we sat together on the Embankment, still
under police supervision. Once or twice it crossed my mind
that I, an honest citizen, paying rates and taxes, living in a
house and serving on juries, having numerous friends, too,
in the same case, should have forthwith handed young
Alf over to a passing policeman and demanded that he
should thereafter eat skilly and pick oakum.

But that would have been a despicable proceeding. As a
good citizen, perhaps, I should have turned traitor. But as
a student of human nature I refused to tear up the human
document which was opening itself before me.

Besides, as you may have guessed already, young Alf is
no fool; he gives away nothing that he cannot afford to
lose. Up to a certain point he is as frank as you please, nor
do I remember to have seen a touch of shame on his face
during any of his revelations, except when he told me how
he blackmailed a pair of lovers who were talking inno-
cently on Clapham Common. Even from young Alf's point
of view blackmailing is rather bad form, and only to be
resorted to when you haven't one copper to rub against
another. He has described localities, and hinted at dates;
but if I were put into the witness-box and invited to testify
against young Alf in the dock, I do not think I could do
him much harm. Finally, young Alf trusted me.

And so the policeman walked to and fro, flashing his
lantern periodically upon one of the most incorrigible
scamps in London, and passed peacefully on to worry
cabmen.

Young Alf continued his tale with many jerky silences, pulling violently at his cigar, and now and then puffing with amusement at the recollections revived.

It was the memory of the slavey that amused him especially.

'Such bleeders they are – slaveys,' said young Alf, in parenthesis.

Well, young Alf sat in the coffee-shop, enjoying his snack, with a warmth of pride glowing at his heart. For now at last he was in for something class. He was waited on by a girl, a rather nice girl, with pretty hair and pleasant eyes, and that sweet way about her that makes you yearn to shove her off the pavement when you meet her out walking in the street.

She had but lately left school. So she confided in young Alf as he made his meal. And that was a link between them. Young Alf, as you know, was very young at the time. But even on that evening I understand that he was a bit saucy, being precocious. For, of course, he had a big job on hand, and thought a deal of himself. And Alice – that was her name – Alice was compelled to box his ears.

In due time Jimmy returned with the tools, paid for young Alf's meal, and said it was time to start.

Young Alf told Alice that he would look in again when he was passing. Alice replied that she would not break her heart in the meantime; and the two partners started for their job.

On the way down to Denmark Hill, Jimmy explained to young Alf that the job was nothing out of the ordinary. The house was a pretty big one, but, the family being away, it was tenanted by a single slavey who slept on the second floor. Jimmy had spent some days in acquiring this knowledge, and, having acquired it, regarded the job as good as done.

'Jimmy knowed the 'ouse jest as if he'd lived in it a monf,' said young Alf.

At Denmark Hill the railway goes under the roadway. The house that Jimmy had waxed stood near the point at which the railway disappears, and a little back from the road. The pair slipped round to the back, and in a few minutes Jimmy had the kitchen window open, and the house was at their mercy.

They mounted the stairs – by the banisters, of course, Jimmy first, and climbing with some difficulty, young Alf behind, a little nervous. It was the first time he had done anything so big as this; for fanlight-jumping does not count.

At this point young Alf warmed to his story; he threw away his cigar and leaned forward with his elbows upon his knees, speaking in quick, low tones.

'Soon as we got to the second landing, Jimmy stopped and catched 'old of my arm. I don't fink I was scared – not what you'd call scared – an' there wasn't anyfink to be afraid of. But when you're on a job like that in the dark, and 'ave to keep as quiet as you can, it's – it's creepy. See?

'Jimmy says to me in a whisper, "First fing," 'e says, "get that old duck-footed slavey wiv a sneezer." And then I see we was in for a bit of gagging.

'Well, Jimmy knowed awright which room the gal was sleepin' in, an' 'e turned the 'andle wivout a sound, an' 'fore you could turn round we was inside an' creepin' up to the bed. The gal was in a sound sleep and never stirred. Jimmy was 'cross the room quicker'n anyfink; he wes corpylint, Jimmy was, but 'e could walk as light as me, an' I didn't weigh more'n seven stone then – not that. Like lightnin', Jimmy 'ad 'er teef apart an' whipped a piece of wood 'tween 'er jores, – piece of wood about an inch an' a quarter long, an' 'arf as thick froo. Then 'e brought the two straps back, an' fastened 'em be'ind the slavey's 'ead

wiv a buckle. Sing out? She 'adn't no time to sing out.
Jimmy'd got the gag in 'fore she knowed she was awake,
Jimmy 'ad. Jimmy always said that beat all uvver ways of
stopping rat-traps, an' 'pon me soul I b'lieve 'im. It was a
smawt bit of work, that was. But Jimmy didn't fink anyfink of that. Nuffink at all.

"Course, be that time, bein' 'andled like that the slavey
was wide awake. 'Arf out of bed, an' 'arf in, she was, an'
givin' us a look – well, I never see such a look in all me life –
much as to say, "Oh, don't, please; spare me life." An'
then she put up 'er 'ands, like as if she was praying for us to
stop it. Gawblimey!'

Young Alf had to pause for a bit. The reminiscence was
so amusing. Then he leaned back in the seat, shoved his
hands deep into his trouser pockets, which are cut diagon-
ally, and very high.

'Jimmy wouldn't stop for anyfink, Jimmy wouldn't,'
continued young Alf. 'Not when he 'ad a job on. I fink I
was raver sorry for the poor gal meself. Well, Jimmy, 'e
give the slavey a shove an' sent her 'arf way 'cross the
room. "Git back, you bloomin' old cow," says Jimmy.
Then he teared a long strip off of one of the sheets, and
bound the slavey's 'ands togevver, an' tied 'em to the
bedstead.

' 'Course, after that there wasn't anyfink more to fear,
and Jimmy an' your 'umble 'ad the place at their own
sweet will. Reg'lar beano it was that night, wiv no error.
We went right froo the 'ouse, 'cause Jimmy knew all about
it, an' where everyfink was kep. You understand Jimmy'd
been larkin' wiv the slavey when 'e was strollin' about
Denmark Hill, on'y he soon see she wasn't no good. What I
mean, she wasn't game to lend a 'and. See?

'Well, we got togevver about as much swag as we could
scoot wiv, an' a bit over for luck. Then we 'ad a bit of
supper downstairs, quiet an' peaceful, an' a glass of beer

each. Jimmy don't 'old wiv drinkin'. Never did. An' then we come out by the front door wiv as much swag as we could carry, an' a bit over. So we planted some of it in a field 'andy, so's we could lift it some uvver evening. An' lift it we did, s' 'elp me. Fair old beano, that was. Straight.'

He threw back his head and sniffed the river breeze. A tug snorted by, kicking the water viciously from its bows. From the clock tower at Westminster Big Ben spoke.

Young Alf followed the tug with his eyes as he buttoned his coat.

'But what do you suppose became of the slavey?' I asked.

Young Alf sniffed once or twice, and rose from the seat.

'Dessay she 'ad a pretty bad time of it,' he replied. 'But the gag doesn't make anyone peg out, an' if it did, I don't fink Jimmy'd 'ave cared much. Jimmy was about the last man to fink that anyone could stan' 'tween 'im an' a job 'e'd set 'is 'eart on. Well, so long.'

The next moment he was a dim figure walking swiftly and silently away from me up the Embankment.

7
Honest Employment

'What you fink of me bein' a tiger to a toff?' said young Alf, suddenly.

The idea was somewhat grotesque; and possibly my face betrayed me.

'I was. No kid,' said young Alf. 'Reg'lar smart young tiger I was, wiv buttons all down me front. See?'

It was one of those evenings on the edge of winter which makes you disbelieve in the English climate and dream of eternal autumn. We had gone down together to see a boxing-match in Lambeth, a match which was to be one of a series extensively advertised in the houses about the Walk. The pleasant room contained a notice in a prominent place over the mantelpiece. But circumstances had intervened. To put it plainly, the star of the evening had got into the usual difficulty, and was not allowed bail.

As the star was obscured, the minor lights scattered up and down the Walk, explaining how they would have fought and conquered had not fate snatched from them the opportunity; give them just half a chance and he would want a whole hospital to himself. Such were the boasts of the Walk. For the boxing saloon was closed for the evening, and 'Mugs' – by that name we knew the proprietor – was wandering among licensed premises, and becoming more obscene and less intelligible as the evening advanced.

Young Alf, disappointed of the fight, and solicitous for my entertainment, raked his memory for stories.

It appears that when young Alf had been associated with Jimmy for about a week, his mother bethought herself of her maternal responsibilities. As her son wore good clothes, never asked her for money, had no visible means of subsistence and kept irregular hours, it is probable that she had her suspicions. Anyhow, she insisted that young Alf should obtain honest employment. Now this, as young Alf had already pointed out to me, was not an easy thing to do, and when done was scarcely worth the trouble of doing.

However, with all his faults, – and by this time you will have gathered that our young friend is but an imperfect creature, – young Alf was always a good son to his mother. So, in deference to her wishes, he began the search. A butcher's boy, with whom he had a casual acquaintance, happened one day to mention that there was a vacancy in the household of a toff at Clapham Common. Young Alf determined to fill it.

With great care he composed a character of himself, which Jimmy copied out, being an excellent scholar. The character was so good that young Alf was engaged on the spot. His mother was much pleased; even Jimmy expressed approval of the new departure, and promised to come over one day and look young Alf up at Clapham Common.

So with a new name, a new address, and a new character, young Alf entered upon his new duties, which he discharged to the complete satisfaction of his employer.

A few days after the advent of young Alf a new servant arrived at the house on Clapham Common, a circumstance which gave a suggestion to young Alf. For the new servant came from the country, and was as green as the cabbages which grew in her mother's back garden.

Young Alf began tea-leafing.

Now by no stretch of language can tea-leafing be called class. But as a county cricketer, if he can get nothing better to do, will play tip-cat, so young Alf went in for tea leafing to fill up the time. His mistress made very nice milk scones. Tins of cocoa were easy of access. A packet of tea now and again would not be missed. These, with other odds and ends, did young Alf make up into parcels and convey to his mother. As I have said, he was always a good son. Let us remember that when we are inclined to condemn some of his practices.

It soon became evident that someone was laying fingers pretty freely on the domestic stores, and, of course, suspicion fell on the new servant. For young Alf had carefully refrained from tea-leafing until her coming. As he had foreseen, the servant was chucked her job; the mistress thinking that she gave the things to her sister, a big country girl who called about twice a week.

As young Alf told me of his spell of honest employment we were standing at the top of the Walk, where it bends round to meet the Lambeth Road. There is a shop at that point which always interests me. If I shut my eyes and think of something I do not want and could not in any probable circumstances want, and then open them on that shop window, I shall see the thing itself.

A silk hat of the later eighties? It is there. A Jumbo Entertainer's voice producer? It invites you. A bust of Wordsworth – engraved? You may have it at a sacrificial price. 'Law's Serious Call'? It stares you in the face, with 'The Young Criminal' as next-door neighbour. Racing calendars, too, seven years old, and looking their age, you may get; accordions, and briar-pipes, well-coloured, and marked at twopence. It would pay a discontented man to come to that corner – he could ride there from any reasonable part of London for threepence at the outside – and learn how many things he does not want. Where do these strange things come from? And have they any future? You would think that the silk hat of the later eighties would have had enough of life and be glad of oblivion.

I was interested in the shop; but courtesy demanded that I should attend to my entertainer.

'It was rather unfair to the servant, wasn't it?' I remarked.

Young Alf replied, in effect, that he could not afford to let such considerations influence his line of action.

'I got meself to fink about,' he said, using his customary formula. 'The slavey was awright,' he continued. 'I knowed that well enough. She never went sideways. But I 'ad to let 'er go 'cause I'd a bigger job in me eye than sneakin' the small fings. See? Jimmy come over one afternoon an' put 'is lamps over the show. I told 'im there was a good bit of stuff to be got an' Jimmy went away to fink of the best way to land it. But I fort I'd do somefink on me own. See? Look ere!'

Young Alf's face was a miracle of slyness as he touched my arm and drew my eyes to his own.

'I dropped nickin',' he said, 'knowin' I'd be rumbled if I went on when the servant got the chuck, an' I waited till me and the uvver new slavey that come was pretty fick. She took a wunnerful fancy to me, that slavey did, an' when I pitched 'er a tale that my muvver was very poor an' 'ow she lived I didn't know, she was fair gone on the story. Tender-'earted gal she was, an' she fort a lot of me.

'Well, one day the master and the missus went off to Brighton for a short 'oliday, leavin' me an' the slavey to take care of the 'ouse. Soon as they'd gone I rang in my tale to the slavey 'ow my muvver was starvin' in a garret wivout anyfink to eat, an' she wrote out a order to the grocer that supplied the 'ouse, – butter an' eggs an' uvver fings that she fort would be good for my muvver. She said on the order that the fings were to be sent by the boy that'd wait. An' so I did wait, wiv the pony trap, an' soon as I got the parcels off I drives to my muvver's.

'But that wasn't the job I'd got me eye on; don't you go

finkin' that. 'Fore the toff and 'is missus 'd been away free days I rang in anuvver tale 'ow there was a lot of fings in the 'ouse that we could sell an' share the money between us. At first she wasn't game, finkin' we was sure to be rumbled. But I showed 'er the job was as easy as anyfink, an' I could do anyfink wiv that slavey, I could. So we went froo the drawers and broke open the boxes, an' got pretty nigh a cart-load of stuff, which I took an' planted wiv the fence that lived underneaf my muvver's.'

'And what happened,' I asked, 'when your master came back from Brighton?'

'Didn't wait to see,' he replied. 'Next day I saw the slavey off wiv her box from Clapham Junction, and paid 'er fare to 'er 'ome in the country. An' I never set eyes on 'er again, – nor the boss neither. I should say 'e was a bit of a 'ook 'isself, from the swag 'e 'ad about the 'ouse.'

I am bound to say that this seems to be the only evidence against the character of young Alf's late employer.

'The girl that got the sack for tea-leafin' that she never did, got a bit of 'er own back, I reckon,' continued young Alf, 'even if she didn't know it. The missus couldn't be orf finkin' when she found the tiger an' the new slavey'd slung wiv the lot.'

'And the new slavey had a little something on which to start life again,' I suggested.

Young Alf looked sideways at me, with a gleam of amusement in his eyes. His cheeks puffed out. He dropped the stump of his cigar and crushed it under his heel. 'She never fingered a bleed'n' farden,' he said.

8

The Burglar and the Baby

The scheme for obtaining honest employment had broken down. But Jimmy was much pleased with young Alf's exploit; and it must be said that this does infinite credit to Jimmy, who was not devoid of generous feeling. For there is no doubt at all that Jimmy had intended to have his share in the contents of the house on Clapham Common, and he would have been quite justified in resenting the conduct of young Alf in getting all the swag for himself. Jimmy, however, chose to be magnanimous. He was the best pal that young Alf ever had, as young Alf has frequently borne witness, and he promptly invited our young friend, who had advantageously exchanged his livery for a less conspicuous dress, to enter his regular service, which young Alf accordingly did.

Jimmy treated young Alf, who was still an inexperienced hand, with great consideration, and looked about for a job which he could work more or less on his own.

Now, in the course of his walks, Jimmy had noted a house that seemed just the thing for young Alf to try his hand upon. It was situated at Brixton, and Jimmy suggested that young Alf should see what he could do with it.

You will admit, when you have heard the story as young Alf told it to me, that he came out of the affair with some credit to himself.

'Jimmy'd found out all about the fambly,' said young Alf. 'There was a toff an' 'is missus, an' a baby, an' there was free servants, one of 'em the baby's nurse. 'Course Jimmy know'd what time they 'ad their tuck in the evenin'.

' "They'll be downstairs settin' in the dinin'-room," says
Jimmy, as we went along Brixton way. "Best fing you can
do is to go froo the rooms on the first floor, 'cause you can
get up easy, and get down easy if you 'ave to scoot. From
what I unnerstand," says Jimmy, "you'll strike the
missus's bedroom, and don't you forget the jool-cases.
See?"

'I didn't feel very slippy over the job, but Jimmy, 'e
said 'e'd be at 'and if I had to cut for it, an' give a whistle
when I 'ad a chance to grease off. See?

'Well, it was about nine o'clock when I got on the job,
an' me an' Jim sneaked froo the groun's, an' got underneaf a bedroom windy that Jimmy said was the right one
to try.

'There was some wood-work for trainin' flahers agin the
wall, an' Jim, 'e says, "Up you go, cocky," Oh! I didn't tell
you that Jimmy 'e gave me 'is barker 'fore that.'

'But I thought burglars, as a rule, went unarmed, to
avoid temptation,' I interposed.

'Twasn't loaded,' said young Alf, 'wouldn't 'a bin worf
my while to out a bloke. It was different wiv Jimmy.
Jimmy couldn't afford to be lagged again, an' he didn't
mean to, neiver.'

Young Alf's mouth was working in excitement at the
reminiscence.

' "Up you goes," says Jimmy, an' I gets up on 'is
shoulders an' catches 'old of the lath-work, an' pulls meself
up two foot or so, an' then I could lay me 'and on the
windy-sill. In arf a mo I was on the sill, settin' easy, an'
feelin' at the sash. That was fastened up tight. But I'd got
a bit o'putty on me; so I got it out an' put it on the glass
an' whipped a di'mond round it. See?'

'That's the dodge, is it?' I said.

'You can do it that way,' said young Alf, 'or you can do
it wiv a pin if you 'aven't got a bit o' putty. Jest press wiv

your 'and on the other part, while you turn your di'mond
an' pick the bit out wiv a pin. That's easy.

'Well, I 'ad a bit out big enough to get me 'and froo,' he
continued, 'an' I pushed back the catch, an' in arf a tick
I was inside. I was inside, wiv no error, an' there wasn't no
mistake about it either. I 'adn't got more'n 'arf across the
room when I 'eard a orful strange noise, jest like chokin'.'

'Choking?' I exclaimed.

'Chokin', you unnerstand,' he said. 'There was a glim
burning in the room, and I fort it was empty. But jest as I
was nipping across to the door, meanin' to stick a wedge,
you unnerstand, I 'eard a orful strange noise. Didn't take
me long to tumble what it was. There was a youngster, not
more'n free monfs old, in a cot in the corner of the room,
fair bein' strangled. I steps up quiet, and there was the
little bleeder gettin' black in the face froo its night-dress
bein' tied too tight round its gargler. See?

'Well, I out wiv my sticker in a mo an' whipped the
little nipper out o' the cot, an' slashed the string froo, an'
it give a sort of – a sort of—'

Young Alf's mouth was working violently, and he
sought for the word.

'Sob,' I suggested.

'Gobbed, like,' he said, and drew his sleeve across his
mouth. 'Layin' over my arm it was, an' all of a sudden it
set up 'owlin'. That's 'ealfy, I finks, wiv me in a strange
'ouse. Oh yus, it was a bit of awright, it was; specially when
the slavey ran into the room, an' see me wiv the kid in one
'and an' the sticker in the uvver. 'Course she fort I was
goin' to put the little bleeder's lights out, an' she gave a
scream that raised the 'ouse from top to bottom, an' fell
down in a dead faint; an' there was me. Eh?'

I appreciated the awkwardness of the situation; and
young Alf continued:

'I didn't 'ave fair time to look round 'fore in rushes the

guv'nor an' made at me as if he was goin' for my frottle.
Fair ole treat, wasn't it? Me wiv the kid over me arm.
See? Well, I whipped out me bull-dog wiv six teef, an' I
calls out, " 'Nuvver step and your number's up," plain as
I could. 'Course the barker wasn't loaded, but it 'eld 'im
up proper; an', jest as he was stannin' an' lookin' at me an'
the kid, 'is wife come in runnin' an' screamin' like mad.
So I turned the barker on 'er an' 'eld 'er up sharp, an' she
fair goes off on the floor like the slavey. Reg'lar beano, it
was, wiv no error. Me there wiv the kid on me arm – Gawblimey! it was a treat. Eh? But be that time there was
on'y the guv'nor to talk to, an' 'e was lookin' as if 'e wanted to get at my frottle. "What you mean," he says,
"comin' into my 'ouse? What's the meanin' of it?" So I
puts my barker on 'im an' I says, "Carm yourself," I says,
"an' I'll tell you what saved your 'ouse from being bur-
gled." Then I told 'im jest 'ow it was. 'Ow I'd nipped in at
the windy after his stuff, an' found the kid chokin', an' my
'eart'd gone out to the little fing, an' I'd looked more to
savin' its life than gettin' the swag that was in me 'ands,
as you might say.

' "I s'pose," I says, "the slavey fort I was goin' cut the
young 'un's 'ead off when I was snickin' the tape; but you
can see for yourself," I says, "what I done."

'I never see a man so pleased, not in all me life; an' be
that time the missus'd come to, an' took the kid an' 'ugged
it, an' cried over it fit to break 'er 'eart.

'The guv'nor arst me if I'd take anyfink. But I fort 'e
might be on for makin' a spring, so I kept the barker on 'im
an' I says:

' "None o' your old swank, boss," I says. "If you go
crooked I'll 'ave your wall-paper orn'minted wiv your
brains. You ac' fair over the kid, an' I'll clear." Well then
'e called for some wine, an' poured out a couple of glasses.
One of 'em 'e tasted 'imself, so's to show me it wasn't

fiddled, I s'pose. The uvver one I 'ad, wiv what was left in the bottle. An' I could do wiv a gargle. That slavey's scream was enough to scare a bloke till 'is dyin' day, an' don't you make no mistake. 'E was a nice, pleasant gent, the guv'nor was. Seemed as if he couldn't fank me enough for savin' the kid's life. Arrever, when I'd finished what there was in the bottle, I said I fort I must be goin'. So the toff come downstairs wiv me 'an give me a jimmy, an' showed me out of the front door, an' told me never to show my nose round that 'ouse again. Nor I never did.'

Jimmy, who was strolling to and fro outside, was considerably surprised to see young Alf apparently in friendly relations with the master of the house he had just entered by the window. And when he heard the story, and learned that young Alf had got no more than a sovereign by his exploit, Jimmy was fair knocked. Nevertheless he allowed that young Alf had played his hand as best he could under the circumstances, and took him on as his regular mate, putting him up to about as many quiffs in crib-cracking as any boy ever got inside his napper.

9
The Coming of Love

Young Alf, as you have been given to understand, was precocious, having been brought up in a society which will tolerate everything but incompetence, and having struck out a line for himself as soon as he had escaped from the schoolroom; wherefore you will conclude, and conclude rightly, that love came early into the life of young Alf.

The conscientious reader will already have caught the first faint flushes of the great passion which heralded the dawn of young Alf's manhood. He has, I gather, been loved by many, and loved more than one. Many names of many girls float across his reminiscences; some of them are to me – and, I fear, to him – mere names, and nothing more. As is the case with the rest and the best of us, young Alf climbed to the height of his desire over his mistakes. And his mistakes were not few. As a ladder they should raise him high.

Of many of these flames I cannot find even the ashes. But there was the girl he invited to drive with him to the Derby; the girl who helped him to nick the toff's property in the bar; and there was Emmamarier.

You must not miss the story of Emmamarier, for it is one upon which young Alf looks back with great satisfaction. Also it has a moral attached to it, a moral which needs no pointing.

Love seemed to come with Emmamarier, who had, I presume, her attractions. Anyhow, she attracted young Alf. Also she attracted Maggots, who was an acquaintance of young Alf's.

Now Maggots was employed in sitting at the tail of a

van, and doing odd jobs about a warehouse in the Borough.
Thus his days were occupied and his evenings left free for
dalliance. At this period, as you know, young Alf had his
days to himself, but was frequently engaged in the evening.

Also Emmamarier was a flirt.

The plot develops obviously.

For Emmamarier permitted her lovers to overlap. One
evening young Alf, who sometimes took an evening off,
was turning from Vauxhall into Tyers Street, on his way to
Lambeth Walk, when he encountered Emmamarier in
company with Maggots. There was a bit of an argument;
not enough of an argument to cause a window in Tyers
Street to open, but enough to black one of Maggots' eyes,
and to send Emmamarier scurrying up the street.

The situation was awkward.

Both boys wanted Emmamarier. And Emmamarier
wanted both boys.

But neither boy was satisfied with fifty per cent of
Emmamarier.

Nor would Emmamarier have been contented with fifty
per cent of both boys.

As days passed the situation became intolerable. For
Maggots and young Alf met constantly, both being on the
watch for infidelity; and Emmamarier did not know which
of the two she was walking with.

Advice came from various friends. The advice was taken,
and young Alf and Maggots decided to fight for Emmamarier. Moreover, Emmamarier, when the scheme was
laid before her by Maggots, consented willingly, stipu-
lating only that she should be permitted to watch the
fight.

On this condition she promised to belong to the winner.

The condition was accepted. The preliminaries were
simple and easily arranged. One of the stables off Lambeth Walk, in which many a quiet scrap has taken place,

was selected as the scene of the conflict. Three trusty friends were invited to see fair; and young Alf and Maggots stripped to the waist, while Emmamarier, the prize, sat proudly on a rung of the ladder which led to the loft, and waited for the victor to claim her.

The fight was soon over, for half-way through the second round young Alf knocked Maggots out, and sent for beer. Maggots recovered his senses as soon as the beer came, and handed over Emmamarier formally to young Alf.

And here a strange thing happened: for young Alf, having won Emmamarier, no longer desired her. He told Maggots that a girl who wanted to be fought for was not worth having, and that he resigned all claim on Emmamarier in favour of Maggots; whereupon Maggots, not to be outdone in generosity, declared that he would have no truck with her.

So Emmamarier was taken by the shoulders, cleared ignominiously out of the stable, and got no beer.

Young Alf and Maggots put on their coats, had a friendly drink together, and ever since then have been the best of pals, having frequently been associated in little jobs to their mutual profit.

But that was not real love. Real love came to young Alf when he encountered Alice in the coffee-shop, to which he frequently recurred in order to enjoy for a season the pleasure of Alice's society. That this was real love is certain enough. For whereas young Alf, as we have seen, objected to fighting for Emmamarier, he did not, as we shall see, mind fighting for Alice.

We were talking one evening of foreigners – a class of person for which young Alf has a great contempt – and the subject led him to a story in which he figures as the champion of virtue in distress. It shows, too, how he first captured the imagination of Alice.

We were sitting in the saloon-bar of the house at the

corner of Paradise Street – The Feathers. The bar was almost empty. It contained but one customer except ourselves, a man who spoke with a pronounced German accent.

Young Alf rolled an eye after the man as he left the bar.

'There's too many of them foreigners about,' said young Alf, as the door swung to and fro and settled to rest, cutting off the din of the Walk from our ears. 'Too many be 'arf. Ef you was to arst me, I wouldn't 'ave 'em in the country. They're no bleed'n' good.'

'Have you ever worked with a foreigner?' I asked.

Young Alf's mouth and shoulders expressed violent dissent.

'I'd never 'ave a foreigner workin' wiv me,' he said. 'Nor I don't believe any boy that's worked the biz down our way'd take on a foreigner. Soon as you get in a 'ole a foreigner shows the white feaver and turns round on yer. See?'

Young Alf leaned suddenly forward, elbows on knees, his mouth working, and I knew that another reminiscence was struggling for expression.

'Didn't I never tell you about that Frenchy that we bashed?' he asked, with a swift, sidelong glance.

I replied that the story would be new to me.

'Well, I told you 'bout Alice – ow I larked wiv 'er in the cawfy-shop.'

I remembered Alice.

'Lived down China Walk, Alice did. Pretty little gal wiv yellow 'air – none o' your bloomin' faked actris kind o' tow – but real golden, – straight. Reg'lar little pride of the place Alice was, an' everybody liked 'er. Only I flatter myself she liked me more'n she liked anybody else. See? Well, Alice was slavey at the cawfy-shop – I told you that. An' one night me and Scrappin' Dick was comin' by the cawfy-shop togevver—'

'Scrapping Dick? Who was he?' I asked.

'Fort I told you 'bout 'im,' said young Alf. ''E come into the gang just after what I did. I expect Scrappin' Dick'd took on pretty nigh every boy in the Walk, from first to last, an' turned 'is face into a butcher's shop too, wiv no error. 'E won't do much scrappin' not for anuvver two years or so; doin' a stretch 'e is. But I'm told 'e's got a nice little bit o' stuff planted 'gainst the time when he comes out again.'

'Well, what about Alice – and—'

'We was comin' by the cawfy-shop where Alice was slavey, me and Scrappin' Dick, an' there was Alice stannin' outside on the pavement, sobbin' fit to break 'er little 'eart.

'An' no wunner she was sobbin', 'cause when we stopped and arst 'er what was the matter, she tells us the boss of the 'ouse – 'e was a Frenchy, 'e was – the boss of the 'ouse'd been tryin' to interfere wiv 'er. I arst 'er what 'e'd been doin' of; but she wouldn't say no more than 'e'd been interferin' wiv 'er, and went on sobbin' somefink cruel. Dick he turns round an' 'e says:

' "Look 'ere, we ain't goin' to see the girl wronged by a bloody frog-eater, eh?"

'I'd made up me mind a'ready, on'y I was finkin' what was the best way to snuff 'im. "Same 'ere," I replies to Dick. "I'm going to see young Alice righted, and that's all about it. Come on," I says.

' "I'm wiv you," says Dick.

'An' wiv that in we goes togevver, an' young Alice stannin' all the time on the pavement outside.

'We reckoned we'd 'ave a snack 'fore getting to work, specially as we didn't mean to pay for it – not in the usual way. So we called for a small do an' two doorsteps each, an' the Frenchy come an' brought it to us. I could see Alice's yellow 'air outside where she was stannin', but she wasn't cryin' no more then. She was peerin' round the door to see what we was goin' to do. I was finkin' of 'er more'n I was finkin of me snack. Well, when we'd done, Dick started arstin' the Frenchy about Alice bein' interfered wiv; an' 'e puts 'is shoulders up an' says:

' "Vat is it you to business wiv me?" That's their bleed'n lingo, y' know. "You b'lieve vat girl?" says the Frenchy. "Yes we do, you bloody frog-swallerer!" I chips in.

'Then Dick says: "Let's give 'im a one two," 'e says. But the Frenchy ran back to the parlour be'ind the shop, and in 'arf a mo 'e'd brought out a dam savage-lookin' bull-terrier, that made as if 'e was goin' to make a go for us. So, quicker'n you could say knife, I leans over an' gets 'old of a bottle, an' lands out. Slashed the dawg clean across the dial, I did, an' carved 'is front pretty well in two. The dawg ran froo to the back wiv a terrible 'owl, an' I turned round to see what Dick was up to. An' there was Dick puttin' the Frenchy over the tables an' chairs proper. He could do that, Dick could, wiv no error. Then I come in, and sent 'im down into the sawdust by way of givin' 'im a change of diet. Fair knockout that'd 'a' been for the froggy, on'y jest as I'd got 'is razzo into one of the sputtoons young Alice comes runnin' in, an' callin' that the missus'd gone for the cops.

'Well, I fort it was about time for us to clear, an' I scooted quick as I could; nor I didn't see no cops at all. But a couple of 'em come along and pinched Dick just as 'e was comin' out of the cawfy-shop. Wasn't much good Dick sayin' anyfink with the froggy layin' there, an' is ole mag in the sputtoon. Eh? So next day Dick was up in front of the beak for a murd'rous assault. 'Ealfy, wasn't it? An' 'im on'y takin' it out of the bleed'n' Frenchy what was inter-ferin' wiv young Alice. S' 'elp me! Well—'

Speech failed young Alf for the moment. He leaned back in his seat with his hands thrust deep in his pockets, an

attitude which necessitated the hunching of his shoulders.
His eyes blazed with the excitement of the narrative, and
his cheeks worked like the cheeks of the puff-adder.

'What'd you 'a' done if your young lady'd been interfered wiv?' asked young Alf presently.

I expressed the heartiest appreciation of his conduct,
and inquired of the subsequent fate of Scrapping
Dick.

'Well, next day Dick was up before the beak,' continued
young Alf, relaxing somewhat the tension of his manner.
'An' me an' the uvver boys was in the p'lice court to 'elp
pull 'im froo.'

'Was Jimmy there?' I asked.

'Jimmy wasn't there,' replied young Alf. 'Jimmy never
did 'old wiv scrappin' and makin' yourself conspickyus.
But young Alice fried it up for the Frenchy pretty warm,
an' told the beak about 'is interferin' wiv 'er, an' 'ow she'd
told Dick, makin' no mention of me, you unnerstand,
though there was me stannin' where the beak could put 'is
lamps over me, carm as you please. But the froggy got all
the best of it all froo, an' Dick 'ad it weighed out to him to
the tune of forty bob, or a month. Course the brass was
made up by the uvver boys before Dick got took to the
stir.'

The saloon bar was filling, and young Alf was looking
under his brows at a quietly-dressed man who was leaning
against the corner of the partition and smoking a cigar.
The quietly-dressed man seemed interested in nothing but
his cigar, unless it was the shoes of his neighbours.

Young Alf shot a glance at me.

'That's a split,' he said.

'How do you know a detective when you see him!' I
asked.

'Know 'im?' said young Alf, sniffing contemptuously.
'Be lookin' at 'im.'

'Well, anyway,' I said, 'the story ends well. And I suppose Alice was very proud of you?'

Young Alf wagged his head.

'I don't meanter say there was anyfink to talk about – me takin' on a Frenchy an' 'is dawg. But what I meanter say is this: us boys don't often get a chalk down in their favour, but that time a couple of us saw to it that the bleed'n' foreigner don't always get the best cut off the joint in this country. Eh? They mustn't try any of their old hank just as they please when any of us boys is around an' about. Tell you what it is, there's a dam sight too many of them foreigners in the country, Hightalians an' Frenchies an' the rest of 'em. Too many be 'arf. Mor' 'n that.'

We parted at the door of The Feathers, and young Alf slid suddenly from my view.

He has a wonderful way of disappearing; a keen eye for cover. One moment he stands in full sight before you, the next moment he is not.

10

On Pitching a Tale

'Anybody ever arst you what I am?' said young Alf suddenly, as we walked in the Westminster Bridge Road. ''Cause you know what to say if they do?'

'I should say you were a friend of mine,' I replied.

'That wouldn't do,' replied young Alf. 'I shouldn't be 'arf seprized if a split that'd seen me wiv you come to you an' arst after my occupation. 'Awse-plaiter. That's what you say. I'm a 'awse-plaiter – see? You bear me out?'

I undertook to remember.

Whereupon young Alf proceeded to moralize and to point his moral with a tale.

'You got to 'ave your tale ready,' he said. 'You're awright if you pitch your tale wivout 'esitating, an' your tale's as good as anybody else's, 'specially if you ring it in first an' get somebody to bear you out. That's right, ain't it?'

It seemed right. But I did not wish to interrupt the current of his reflections. So I remained silent.

'Don't you believe it?' said young Alf, with a sharp look round at me. 'Then I'll eggsplain my meanin'. What I mean is, you got to 'ave your tale ready 'fore you start on your job, else when you get pinched what are you goin' to say? Eh?

'Well, when I went wiv Jimmy reg'lar I didn't live wiv my muvver no more. I went an' kipped wiv a pal. Be'ind the kip there was a bit o' yard, wiv a wall that run along at the back of all the 'ouses in the row. One night I'd 'eard about a bit o' stuff I fort I could put me 'ooks on in a 'ouse 'bout six doors up. So when the street was quiet an'

72

the blokes in the kip was mostly asleep, out I nipped an' got on to the wall an' crawled along to the 'ouse I'd marked, wivout makin' any noise. But jest as I was lookin' for me drop into the yard somefink catched 'old of me leg, an' there was a copper that'd crep up in 'is silent shoes. He pulled me down off the wall, an' 'e says:

' "Now then, what's the little game, eh?" 'e says.

'I was fair knocked. 'Cause you understand, I 'adn't got me tale ready to pitch. See? So I made out as if I was cryin', so's to get time to fink. An' then the slop 'e shook me shoulder an' says:

' "Now then, what were you doin' on that 'ere wall?"

'Be that time I'd fort of me tale, so I gives over cryin', and I says:

' "Please, mister p'liceman," I says, "don't you go an' let on to my faver."

' "Your faver," 'e says. "Who's your faver, an' where is 'e?"

' "In there," I says, pointing to free houses furver up the row. "'E's waitin' up for me, an' if he sees me comin' in at the front 'e'd lam me somefink cruel. I know faver," I says.

' "Well, you come along 'er me an' we'll find 'im," says the cop. "I'm not satisfied wiv your explanation," he says.

'So we went round to the front, an' the cop kep 'is 'and on my shoulder, an' knocked at the door. A old man wiv whiskers come an' opened it.

' "'Ello," he says, "what's wrong now."

' "Look 'ere, faver," I chips in; "this yer cop's pinched me 'cause I was comin' in the back way, fear you'd lam me. You won't lam me, will yer? I wasn't on'y 'avin' a lark."

'The old 'un 'e put his lamps over me. "This your boy?" says the cop.

73

' "Jest you lemme get at 'im," says the old 'un. "I'll wail his young skin proper. You lemme get at 'im, that's all."

' "Then that's awright," says the cop. "Want's lookin' after, 'e does. You lay it on fick."

' "Fick's the word," says the old 'un. An' then off goes the copper. Got out o' that awright, didn't I?'

Young Alf's face assumed a look of preternatural cunning.

'But,' I objected, 'that wasn't your father, was it? I thought you told me—'

'What do you fink?' said young Alf. 'Never 'ardly spoke to 'im in me life. On'y he kep' the 'ouse where one or two of my pals kipped, 'mong 'em bein' Maggots. An' I knowed 'e was strite. See? 'E tumbled soon as I called 'im faver. What?'

We walked on for some moments in silence as we crossed the Lambeth Road and turned into the Walk.

'See what I mean 'bout havin' your tale ready?' said young Alf, presently. 'There was anuvver time, when I took Kate wiv me to the Derby in a little cart, an' me lookin' like a toff, wiv no error.'

Young Alf wagged his head at the memory of the drive, and clicked his tongue, as though the pony were still under his hands.

'Kate?' I said, 'I don't think I've heard anything about Kate,'

'Oh, there was more besides Alice,' said young Alf, smoothing out his neckerchief. 'I always kep two or free gals hangin' about. 'Obby of mine, I s'pose.'

We were within hail of the pleasant room, of which you have heard, and I proposed a visit, wishing to hear something more concerning the art of pitching a tale. Young Alf was willing, and we entered.

Three men, who I imagine would be described on the

charge-sheet as commission agents, were sitting and talking quietly at the other end of the room.

Young Alf and I sat apart from them, young Alf giving a swift nod as he dropped into his chair. As usual he took ginger-beer.

It appears that young Alf had struck a streak of luck in the spring of which he spoke. He had got a nice little lot out of a house over at Clapham, which Jimmy had reconnoitred for him. His entrance was effected without difficulty, at about one in the morning. But on the hall table, over which the gas-lamp was burning dimly, he found a note from the lady of the house to its master, stating that she was tired of waiting up and had gone to bed. So young Alf, ascending to the drawing-room upon the first-floor, hid himself in the dark, under the sofa, where he abode until the master of the house returned, extinguished the gas, and mounted to his room, which was on the same floor as the room in which young Alf lay concealed.

Young Alf was delighted to hear the lady of the house begin lecturing her husband on the evil of late hours and bad company, for, though still young in years, he knew that when a capable and energetic woman is rebuking her husband the husband has no leisure to think of anything else.

'First of all,' said young Alf, as he told me the story, 'the old boy took 'is gruelling wivout a murmur; but after a bit 'e put in a word on 'is own, or 'e tried to. Didn't make no 'eadway, though, 'cause more 'e said, more she went on twice as fick wiv 'er ole mag.

'It was jest a bit o' lucky for me, them goin' on like that, 'cause it give me a chance of runnin' froo the rooms, knowin' all the time that the boss'd got 'is 'ands full of more'n 'e could 'andle. So I got froo the job carm an' easy in me mind, an' that's somefink to say thanky for when you're in a strange 'ouse. More'n that, I fort when I'd done

75

that I might as well 'ave somefink downstairs after waitin'
unner the sofy, while the boss was gettin' his tongue-pie
upstairs. See? So I creeps down to the kitchen and does
myself proper wiv corned beef an' pickles. An' all the
time I could hear the ole geezer upstairs layin' it on to
'er ole man fick as she knew 'ow. Well, all said an' done,
I got away wiv about forty pounds worf of cash and
jool'ry.'

But this was not the end of young Alf's luck. Most of his
exploits were carefully planned, and carried out with due
regard to established rules. But now and then a sudden
thought, an inspiration, as it were, came to him; and an
inspiration is often more profitable than a carefully-devised
plan.

This particular inspiration came one Sunday afternoon,
when young Alf and two pals were loafing in a populous
North London street. It was closing time; and young Alf,
being off his accustomed beat, was keeping a sharper
lookout than usual for promises of future gain. He was
not thinking in the least, so he assured me, of the public-
house he was passing when the inspiration came. But he
noticed that the barman was just about to close the door;
and, glancing past the barman, young Alf's quick eye
caught the glitter of several nice little heaps of coin on one
of those tell-tale arrangements that many publicans used
before the introduction of the present automatic type-
writer-phonograph register.

Now, many boys would have passed on unnoticing.
Young Alf's pals passed on. The boy who notices succeeds.
Young Alf notices everything that takes place within three
hundred and sixty degrees of his line of sight.

Not only does young Alf notice; he reflects. On this
occasion he reflected upon the streets he had passed
through, the probable size of the public-house, and its
situation relative to other streets. He inferred back prem-

ises. The inference led him to the further conclusion that a good stroke of business might be brought off.

He slipped away from his companions and retraced his steps, turning into a side street. Here he struck the back premises, entered boldly, noting the lay of the rooms and the passages as he proceeded, and meeting nobody, concealed himself in the room behind the bar. The bar was clear, and there was a hurrying and scurrying for dinner. After waiting for a quarter of an hour or so, young Alf concluded that the household would be well engaged at the dinner-table. It took him but a few seconds to scoop up the morning's takings, which were conveniently placed in heaps, after which he quietly drew the bolts and emerged by the front door. Young Alf thought that this public-house must be doing a good trade, and could well spare the twenty pounds in gold and silver which he removed. He only regretted that the difficulty of suitable transport compelled him to leave the copper behind.

It is young Alf's habit, when he has brought off a job of this kind successfully, to revisit the scene of action at an early date. This is not a weakness, such as impels a murderer to return to the place where his crime was committed. It is rather an instance of his careful regard for details, which has secured for him an immunity from arrest beyond the usual lot of his kind. He wishes to assure himself that he has not incurred suspicion, so that he may walk the street at ease and sleep peacefully at night. Even in so small a matter as that of the centre-bit which he nicked in the Walk while inspecting other articles which he did not require, he did not neglect this precaution. Requiring a centre-bit for the ordinary purposes of burglary, he slipped the implement under his coat while the shopman's back was turned, and then remarking that he had not found what he required, departed; then, having planted the centre-bit, he strolled back and, as though still hesitating over a purchase, ascertained that the centre-bit had not been missed. That done, he put the incident behind him.

So, on the morning following the incident at the public-house, young Alf made his way to North London, and sauntering into the bar, spoke affably with the landlady. In the course of conversation he advised her to keep an eye on suspicious characters, since he had heard that several public-house robberies had been committed in the district. The landlady thanked him, but said that his advice came a day too late. Then she told him what had happened on the previous day – at least, some of it. And young Alf, remarking that you wouldn't think such a lot of money would be kept in the bar at one time, left for Lambeth with a peaceful mind. The landlady had no idea who had stolen the money, or how it had been stolen.

The twenty pounds belonged to young Alf, and there was no cause for further anxiety about it.

Though not invariably just, as we have seen in the case of the slavey whom he defrauded of her share in the swag from the Clapham Common house, young Alf was not infrequently generous. Wherefore, a considerable proportion of the brass he had pinched at the public in North London, as well as of the proceeds of his little haul, of which you read earlier in this chapter, went in standing treat to pals. At that time a favourite meeting-place was in the bar of a public-house off the Westminster Bridge Road, and here many convivial evenings were spent, young Alf putting up the ready to the admiration of his friends and the satisfaction of the landlord. Even the landlord, a genial soul, and a lover of good company, was induced to lower his own liquor at young Alf's expense.

It was during one of these evenings that young Alf, always chivalrous, reflected that Kate should share in his good fortune. To me Kate is little but a name. She was, I understand, one of the smartest fillies in the Walk; also she was engaged, when not otherwise employed, in the manufacture of card-board boxes. This was some time ago. What she is doing now I cannot say.

Young Alf recounted this incident in his career, in order to illustrate his thesis that if you want to go sideways you have got to have your tale ready to pitch. And he told it thus, sipping his ginger-beer at intervals, while the men at the other end of the room continued their conversation, with an occasional glance towards us:

'Well, the landlord had a smart stepper an' a cart, an' one evening I finks to meself it'd be a bit of awright if I took Kate down to the Derby wiv a bit o' class. See? There was the pony eatin' is 'ead off in the stable be'ind, an there was the cart ready an' waitin'. Now, what did I tell you? Didn't I say if you wants a fing you got to go and take it? That's what I done.'

'But how did you do it?' I asked.

Young Alf set down his glass and thrust forth his lips contemptuously.

'Went an' took it. Didn't I tell you? Early next morning, 'fore anyone was about, there was me in the stable at the back of the pub 'arnessing the nag. I got away awright wivout anyone seeing me; wouldn't 'ave worried me off me rocker if they 'ad. 'Cause I'd got me tale ready to pitch.'

'What was the tale?' I asked.

"Arf a mo,' said young Alf. 'I'm comin' to that. Well, Kate was waitin' for me where I'd told 'er, an' in 'ardly no time I was on the road wiv the smartest little filly in the Walk by me side. Goin' fine, we was.'

Young Alf cocked his head, clicked his tongue, and assumed the attitude of one who sits behind a spirited animal and enjoys it. The men at the other end of the room ceased their conversation, and turned to listen to young Alf's narrative.

'Passed everyfink that was goin' down to the Derby, we

did. An' Kate larfin' fit to bust 'erself. Gawblimey! fair old beano it was, wiv no error.'

Young Alf suddenly dropped the attitude of one who drives, and I inferred disaster – rightly.

'About 'arf way to Epsom,' he continued, 'I'd slackened the pace a bit as we come to a stiff bit of hill, an' I got the awfice from a toff that was drivin' 'ard that I was wanted be'ind. 'Course I tumbled at once that the bung'd put the splits on me. What do you fink I did?'

'A scoot,' I suggested. 'Whipped up the pony, outdistanced the detectives, sold the pony and trap at Epsom, put the money on the winners, came back by special train, and married Kate. Eh?'

Young Alf's face denoted scorn.

'Not me,' he said. 'I see I was rumbled, in a manner of speakin.' I'd got a little bit up me sleeve, arrever. See? So, soon as I got the wheeze, I whips the pony round, and trots carm an' peaceful back along the road. Nor I 'adn't got more'n fair started 'fore a couple of splits that I knew come up in a dog-cart. One of 'em caught the pony by the 'ead, an' the uvver nabbed me by the collar. "What you doin' of?" I says, angry-like. An wiv that I got the bracelets on, an' there was me bein' drove back 'ome in the dog-cart; while the uvver split took Kate be'ind the pony. Cryin', Kate was. She didn't know 'ow I'd got the turn-out; an' it fair knocked 'er, me bein' pinched like that.'

'Well, there was no getting out of it that time, was there?' I said, as young Alf paused and looked across towards the men at the other end of the room, who were obviously interested in the story.

'Talk sense,' said young Alf, as one of the men laughed – the man in the brown coat and the red silk muffler. 'Didn't I tell you I'd got me tale ready to pitch? Why, I was larfin' and talkin' wiv the split all the way back to the pub.

' "Awright, cocky," 'e says, "you'll get your show te-morrer."

'Knowed me, 'e did, well as 'e knowed 'is own muvver.

'What's more, I got me show. See?'

Young Alf's mouth and eyes assumed an extraordinary angle.

The man in the brown coat stuck out his legs and leaned back in his chair, contemplating the ceiling, and showing an under-chin that was blue.

'Well, when we got back to the pub I'd got a pretty good chance of spendin' my Derby day wivin four narrer walls,' continued young Alf, whose mouth was working with excitement. 'An', sure 'nough, they caged me for the night. On'y they let Kate go.'

The man in the brown coat and the red muffler was nodding at the ceiling; the other two were leaning forward, listening.

'Next mornin',' continued young Alf, 'there was me up 'fore the beak answerin' a charge of stealin' a 'awse an' trap. 'Ealfy, eh? Specially when the bung come up, an' the splits come up, an' all of 'em put in a peg for me well as they knew 'ow. So when they'd said all they could fink of, the beak turns to me where I stood, you unnerstand, an' 'e arsts me if I wanted to arst any questions. 'Course I wanted to arst any questions. That was me chance. See?'

Young Alf finished his ginger-beer at a gulp, and dashed down the glass upon the table.

' "Yes, your worsh'p," I says, quite pelite, "I should like to arst the prosecutor whether he was sober the night 'fore I took the trap."

'The bung didn't say nuffink, an' the beak 'e looked at 'im an' says my question over again.

' "I arst," I goes on, "I arst the prosecutor if 'e wasn't so drunk the night 'fore I took the trap, that 'e didn't know what 'e said nor what 'e didn't say."

'You should 'a' seen the bung when I put that question to 'im.

'Then the beak says: "The prisoner arsts if you was intoxicated on the previous evenin'. Was that so?"

'An' then I chips in: "Why, he told me, your worship," I says, " 'e told me I was welcome to the trap to go for a drive down the road to the Derby, as 'tween frens," I says; "told me so that very night in 'is own bar."

'Wiv that the beak put 'is lamps over the bung, an' says, solemn as you please, "Was you intoxicated?"

'That fetched the bung, you unnerstand; 'cause there was people in court that'd sin 'im on 'is back time after time froo drink.

' "I must admit I was somewhat overcome," says the bung, lookin' sheepish.

' "Do you remember," the beak goes on, "do you remember everyfink as took place on the night in question, an' more partickerly the time when the prisoner says you promised 'im the loan of your 'awse an' trap?"

'Then the bung 'ad to own up.

' "I can't swear that I'm clear as to everyfink," 'e says.

' "Fact is," says the beak, "you don't seem to know what 'appened, an', bein' a doubt in the matter, it's my duty to discharge the prisoner."

'So I got off. An' 'ow did I get off? Jest 'cause I'd got me tale ready to pitch. I know'd all the time they couldn't prove anyfink against me. Not them.'

'But was the landlord drunk?' I asked.

''E was one of them blokes,' said young Alf, 'that can't never be certain wevver they was drunk last night or wevver they wasn't. See? There's lots like that. An' that's what made me fink of me tale.'

'Then the tale wasn't true?'

Young Alf picked up his glass, which was empty, and looked at it.

'I've 'ad a few turns in the dock,' he said; 'an' I fink it's time the pris'ner 'as a chance of puttin' in 'is bit o' lyin'. Anyfink worse than the perj'ry that goes on in courts – well, strike me, it'd be a tough 'and that'd come up to the form that some of the beaks pass for Gawd's truth.'

The man in the brown coat dropped his eyes from the ceiling, disclosing a rather pleasant face – fat, with a snub nose and a stubbly moustache.

'Sin Jawge litely?' he asked suddenly.

'George? George 'oo?' said young Alf.

'Jawge o' Mitcham,' said the man in the brown coat.

'Oh, 'im,' said young Alf. 'No, nor don't want to it.'

''Aven't bin lookin' for 'im, I reckon,' said the man in the brown coat. ''E bin lookin' for you?'

'Shut yer 'ead,' said young Alf, modestly.

But I could see that his modesty was only assumed.

'I should like to hear about George,' I said.

Young Alf would have another ginger-beer. And he told me of George, while the man in the brown coat stirred something hot in his tumbler, and followed the story with nods and winks, as one who anticipated its points, but enjoyed them as they came.

I I
George of Mitcham

'It wasn't anyfink,' said young Alf. 'On'y there was a lot of the uvver boys there at the time, an' it made a lot of larfin'. It was outside there in the bar, an' me an' Maggots wiv some more pals was stannin' about, an' presently, lookin' 'cross to the uvver side of the bar I got me lamps on to a ole bloke that was talkin' pretty free. Big, good-tempered lookin' chap 'e was, wiv a red face. Up for a 'oliday 'e was, I 'eard him say. Goin' sportin', too, 'e says, else his name wasn't George.

'Wiv that it comes into me 'ead that I'd 'ave a game wiv 'im, so I jest gives Maggots the wheeze, an' 'e says 'e was wiv me, an' then I slides over to where George was stannin'.'

'Was George his Christian name, or his surname?' I inquired.

Young Alf considered a moment.

'I dunno,' he replied. 'Well, I slides up, an' puttin' me 'and out, I says: "'Ello, George," I says, "who'd ever 'a thought of seeing you in these parts!"

'George 'e shakes 'ands and looks round at the comp'ny.

' "I'm pleased to see you," 'e says, "but damme if I can call you to mind."

' "Well, George," I says, "that's a fair knock-out. You comin' up to Lunnun from the ole place an' droppin' in 'ere premiskious, an' meetin' one o' the ole lot an' you don't reckernize 'im. That's a good 'un," I says. "That *is* a good 'un, an' no meestike."

'Wiv that he begins to get uneasy in 'is mind, an' 'e says, "I s'pose I oughter apologize," 'e says.

84

' "S'pose!' I chips in, "you jest take anuvver look at my dial."

' "Why, I rather fancy," 'e says, "now I get anuvver look at you, I've seen you down Mitcham way."

' "Good old Mitcham," I says. "Course you 'ave. What do you fink?"

' "'Pon my word," 'e says, "it's most extraordinary, but I can't recall your name, on'y I know your face well as anyfink."

' "You wait a bit," I says, "an' you'll fink of my name. But what are you goin' to 'ave 'long'er me, George? 'Tain't often I come across a ole fren' from the ole place."

' "No, no, young fellow," says George, "it isn't every day that I gets up to Lunnun, an' when I come it's for a 'oliday. An' wouldn't you? What's yours?' he says, "an' what's gen'l'men all takin'?"

'An' wiv that he orders drinks round, an' I fort it was time to get to work on 'im.

' "'Ow's Mitcham lookin'? I says. "Same as ever?"

' "Not much changed," says George, "not since you left."

'Then Maggots 'e slided up.

' "Fren' o' yours?" says Maggots.

' "Fren' of mine! 'Course 'e is," I says. "Me an' George was old pals."

' "An' what might you be doin' now?" says George.

' "Dealin'," I replies. "An' if you should 'appen across a nice little watch or anyfink like that in the course of your travels, I might be able to do a deal wiv you," I says.

' "Why, you can 'ave this one for fifty bob," says George, pullin' out a nice-lookin' ticker.

' "That's a sight too big for 'im, George," says Maggots.

' "Not a bit of it," says George, "why, you don't get measured for watches up in Lunnun, do you?"

' "I don't fink it's too big eiver," I says. "Just you put

85

it in here, George," I says. "Never 'ad a watch in his life, that cove didn't; an' 'e wants to make out your lever's one of them ole turnips as fick as a Dutch clock."

'An wiv that George slips the watch inside my vest pocket.

' "There, is there any show about that?" he asks.

' "See it a mile away," says Maggots.

Kiddin', 'e was, of course you unnerstand.

' "Well, it hasn't anyfink to do wiv you," I says, wiv a rare put on that seemed to please ole George fine. "Tell you what I'll do," I goes on, "I'll 'ave glasses wiv you, that I'll stan' over there by the door an' you won't be able to tell which pocket the watch is in. On'y you let George put the watch into whichever pocket 'e likes wivout your lookin'. See?"

' "Done!" says Maggots.

'With that I turns round, so's the uvvers couldn't see where George put the watch, an', artful like, 'e slips it into the side pocket of me coat.

' "Now then," says George, "it's glasses round again if you can see the watch."

'Well, I backed up 'gainst the door at the uvver end of the bar, an' somehow or uvver the door opened and I backed out. An' it wasn't more'n two minutes 'fore I'd planted the ticker. See?'

The man in the brown coat nodded at the ceiling.

'Disy!' he said. 'Disy, 'e is, if there ever was one.'

'And whát became of George?' I asked.

'I didn't come back no more that evenin',' replied young Alf. 'But from what they tell me—'

'Jawge got took up,' said the man in the brown coat. 'Began creatin' a disturbance in the bar, an' 'ad to be chucked out. An' then 'e got took up.'

Young Alf's face expressed supreme indifference to the fate of George.

'Haven't been down Mitcham way litely, eh?' said the man in the brown coat.

Young Alf's mouth worked convulsively; but he made no reply. He does not like being chaffed.

'I suppose you'd always select a countryman for a trick like that?' I suggested

'Well, countrymen ain't generally reckoned to be any smarter than they oughter be, but I think they've smartened up a bit lately; on'y the countryman's got a keener lot o' lads to wait on 'im. See? If you try somefink wiv a watch on a countryman he'll generally take it on. Seems a sort of weakness o' theirs. You arst 'im if he wants a nice ticker cheap, a gold watch 'angin' up at five pound an' worf five times the money. An' then you show 'im the ticket, an say 'e can 'ave it for a quid. Chance of a lifetime you tell 'im. More'n 'arf the times 'e'll 'and over the quid.'

'And doesn't he get the watch, then?'

'Not 'im. There ain't no watch, 'cause the ticket's a fake. See?'

'And what about the pawnbroker? Doesn't he take any steps when he finds his tickets are being forged?'

'Oh, 'e don't trouble 'is 'ead, not likely. More'n 'arf likely the fake's been worked be one of the boys that brings 'im nice useful little fings for pledge. See?'

'Where chaps like George tumble,' resumed young Alf, 'is finkin' they'll be safe in a respectable-lookin' 'ouse. Fact is, thieves put in their best work in the respectable-lookin' 'ouses. There's been a lot of improvement lately, too. I don't b'lieve you'd 'ardly find a low-lookin' pub in the 'ole of Lambeth. What you fink of that? You wouldn't fink it was a fake, would you?'

Young Alf brought from his pocket a piece of pasteboard, which precisely illustrated his meaning. It was a pawn-ticket for a watch on which £5 had been lent.

'Where are these things printed?' I asked.

'I dunno,' said young Alf. 'But Lunnun's a very wide place, an' there's some wide people in it, an' don't you forget it.'

As we quitted the room together the man in the brown coat was showing his blue-black under-chin, and remarking that he was a daisy, strike him!

We parted in the street outside. A moment later young Alf touched my arm.

'You won't forget what I was tellin' you about,' he said. "Awse-plaiter. See?'

I promised to remember.

I 2

The Boot-trick and Others

There are plenty of things lying about the world, un-watched, and waiting to be pinched by the boy who keeps his eyes skinned. But you have to jump at them as soon as you see them. Bicycles, for example. Young Alf, noting the turn of fashion, learned the art of bicycling in a backyard, having made the acquaintance of a barber's assistant who possessed a machine.

Knowledge is power – and young Alf's knowledge of the art of bicycling speedily developed into the power of acquiring bicycles of his own. One day an unguarded bicycle attracted his attention. It stood invitingly upon the kerb, looking for a partner. Young Alf mounted, rode slowly, and with many wobbles, until he came to the first corner. Then he turned, and rode at full tilt to a shop he knows. Within ten minutes the bicycle was disintegrated, and its own maker would not have known it. This fake he has worked many times. If the owner sees him wobbling down the street he explains that he is having a lark. His obvious inexperience, his blatant incompetence witness in his favour. If the owner does not see him, there is no need of explanation.

There are, indeed, many ways of picking up a living outside what we may call the legitimate lines of burglary and pocket-picking. Of many of these young Alf has spoken at various times, and they seem worth collecting into a single chapter, as serving to illustrate the axiom which is the ultimate major premise of young Alf's practical syllogism: that things are there to be nicked. The novelist frequently finds it profitable to fill up odd time with

journalism. In the same way the burglar need not be
ashamed to confess that he descends occasionally to till-
lifting and dog-stealing, when no more serious business
engages his attention. Moreover, idleness leads to mischief.
Young Alf is fully aware that the boy who does not keep
himself busy is liable to get into mischief. He will take to
drink and lose his nerve; at the best, he misses opportunities of keeping his hand in and making a bit extra as well.
Do the duty that lies nearest, not asking if it be a small
matter or a big one, and your reward will be many little
bits of splosh. Blackmailing, for instance. It is not young
Alf's regular business. Indeed, he considers himself rather
above that fake, and confesses, with a certain amount of
shame, tempered with amusement, that on two occasions
he worked it, and even on three occasions brought it off.
The simplest method is to spot a gentleman who is speaking with a lady, say in Oxford Street or in Piccadilly, say
at a little past midnight. You threaten to inform his wife.
In one case, the result was five pounds in young Alf's
pocket. Or you may follow up a pair of innocent lovers on
Clapham Common. In three cases out of four there are
obdurate parents, or some reason why the meeting should
not be known. And you can make a bit out of that. But it
is not class; and young Alf – let us do him justice – has
only resorted to blackmailing when very hard pushed for
a crust. And even the best of burglars, if he spends freely
and is generous to his pals, may find himself now and again
hard pushed. Besides, blackmailing is not a wide way of
making a living. For the blackmailer has to disclose his
identity, more or less; and if the victim only has the pluck
to refuse, he needn't pay. Because the blackmailer never
intends to carry out his threat. The game wouldn't be
worth the shoe-leather.

There are, however, numerous other means of turning
spare time to profitable use – means, too, of which no

criminal need be ashamed. For example, there is a rather amusing little quiff which, as it can only be worked during the season of Advent, comes up every year with a pleasing novelty. If you have an evening off, you follow up a party of waits, carefully marking their pitches. Next morning you arise betimes, and calling at the houses you have marked, reap the reward that the waits have earned. You may rely upon it that the waits, having been up half the night, will take an extra hour in bed. It is well to select a melodious party, preferably church choristers singing for a charity, or your only reward may be contumely. An element of humour enters into this fake; for when the genuine waits call later in the day for their money, they are regarded as swindlers.

Another fairly safe way of getting hold of the ready is to collect money at Lifeboat processions or on Hospital Saturdays. The street collections for hospitals have become somewhat discredited of late; but young Alf has a couple of lady friends who used to array themselves as nurses and make a nice little haul. Young Alf himself prefers collecting for lifeboats, because he knows where to obtain a specially made box in the shape of a boat, and that disarms suspicion. But the public is, as young Alf gladly admits, wonderfully credulous. His integrity as a collector was only once challenged. He was getting funds for sending poor children for a happy day in the country. He boldly offered to accompany the doubter to the nearest police station. Of course, he was ready to do a sprint if the offer was closed with. But it was not.

Dog-sneaking, too, though it would scarcely pay as a regular profession, is useful when times are dull. Your objective, of course, is not the dog, but the reward offered for its recovery. And young Alf has picked up many a stray sovereign in this way. He is in the habit, too, of asking a bit extra for the cost of the dog's keep; and he usually gets it. Dog-sneaking is a very safe method of replenishing an empty pocket, for owners never prosecute, even though they may be morally sure that the finder is a thief. They are too delighted at the return of their pet. Besides, they suspect that a prosecution would lead to the poisoning of the animal by the prisoner or one of his pals, and their suspicion is quite justified. Young Alf holds that no boy was ever pinched for dog-stealing.

Burglaries are not often brought off on a Sunday; though I doubt whether this is due to any religious objection on the part of such as young Alf. But a church is an easy mark. The point about a church is that you need not break into it. Young Alf confesses to having robbed three churches, and in each one of them he found a courteous welcome, as well as the loan of certain implements of worship which somewhat embarrassed him. In robbing a church the only difficulty is the breaking out; and that is a small one. Having concealed yourself at the close of the service – an easy matter, since a church affords abundant cover – you have about three hours in which to prise open the offertory boxes. At eleven o'clock, when the police have their eyes on the doors of the public-houses, you may depart in peace. In most cases of church robbery you will read that the offertory-box had not been cleared for some time, and that the precise amount it contained was uncertain.

'Why don't they clear the boxes after each pefawmince?' asks young Alf. And the unanswerable question seems to him his justification.

Buying empty boxes and packing-cases from tradesmen may be made remunerative. The initial expense is small. You want a truck; and the boy who cannot get a truck when he wants it is not called young Alf. Nor is there a lot of kid required for this particular fake; for many shopkeepers are glad to get their cellars cleared of boxes, paper and so forth, especially when a fair price is offered. You gain admittance, you will perceive, to the tradesman's premises, and that is an advantage not to be despised. For even in a grocer's cellar there are things worth having.

The first thing is to collect the empties and make a deal for them. Then you put them together, the smaller inside the larger, so as to save space and make the job a neat one. Say you get half-a-dozen of such cases to put on your truck. It will be very hard if one case that has not been unpacked cannot be shifted with the empties. Let it be something light, – prepared oats, we will say – so that, if stopped, you can apologize: 'Well, I fort it seemed raver 'eavy when I humped it up wiv the empties, on'y it's so dark down there you can't see what you're doin' of.'

On his last box-buying expedition young Alf succeeded in lifting three boxes of oats, which he speedily disposed of to his advantage.

You should keep an eye skinned too for drowsy draymen, for the chain that binds the empty casks together is quite worth having. Young Alf has described to me a little drive he had on the tail of a dray, during which he unfastened nearly a hundred feet of chain, and sold it for three and sixpence.

A boy who wishes to make the most of his opportunities will do well to keep his eye upon such carts and vans as he may encounter. They afford many profitable openings. One day young Alf, going up the Kingsland Road, noticed a big builder's van pull up at a public-house. The driver went inside, and stayed there a considerable time. Young Alf unfortunately could not devise any means of planting a horse and van, as well as a lot of building materials, within any reasonable time; but the chance was too good to be altogether lost. So he sent Maggots, who accompanied him, into the public-house, with instructions to engage the attention of the driver. Young Alf, having noted the address on the van, drove it quietly off to the office. There he explained that he had seen it wandering at large without a driver, and thinking that there might be an accident which would entail loss upon the firm, had taken charge of it. This at considerable inconvenience to himself, and at the expense of a job to which he was making his way. Half-a-sovereign rewarded his enterprise, as well as the offer of the driver's place. He accepted the former; the latter he refused.

But perhaps the smartest thing in cart and van work which young Alf has carried out, was conceived when he noticed that a certain firm in South London was in the habit of sending out large consignments of eggs in cases. He looked up a pal who possessed a pony and barrow, and one morning they started after a van on which about a dozen cases of eggs were loaded. Delivery was to be made in the Clapham district. In the traffic at the Elephant they began to get to work, young Alf on one side and his pal on the other, edging a case inch by inch over the tail board, so as not to make any sudden jerk. For something over a mile they went, patiently helping the case over the edge as opportunity occurred; and then came the ticklish part of the business. Bringing the barrow close up, they raised the box of eggs, and planted it down, as tenderly as if it were a baby, and belonged to them, on their barrow. They turned, and drove for Lambeth, where they arrived without breaking a single egg. Young Alf is proud of this achievement, for wobblers are tricky things to handle. That evening Lambeth Walk saw a cheap line in new-laid eggs, for young Alf was selling them at sixteen a shilling.

But the things that wait for the watchful boy are simply innumerable. You want, we will say, a pair of boots. There are more boots than people in London. And young Alf told me of the boot-trick as we leaned over the parapet of

Westminster Bridge and talked. He was kicking the toes
of those very boots against the stonework as he spoke. It
arose out of a dispute as to the nearest way from Westminster Bridge to Lambeth Walk. I should have gone
down the Westminster Bridge Road, struck the Kennington Road, and turned from Lambeth Road into the Walk.
But young Alf knew a shorter cut.

Besides, he does not go down the Westminster Bridge
Road.

I inquired the reason.

So the story came out.

'It was when me an' Maggots was workin' togevver,'
said young Alf, 'and bofe of us was on the hank for a new
pair of boots. Down on our uppers we was, wiv no error; an'
we 'greed that them trotter cases 'd 'ave to be got, even if
we sneaked 'em. Nor I don't fink Maggots could 'a' walked
easy in a pair of boots that 'e'd 'ad to pay for. Same 'ere,
too. Reg'lar on the make, Maggots was. Well, there was a
ole Jew snob down there that Maggots wanted to get level
wiv.'

Young Alf jerked his head in the direction of the
Westminster Bridge Road.

'Bin Maggots's landlord, 'e had; on'y 'e didn't know it.
See? An' Maggots fort it was time 'e got a bit of his own
back. So we nips down to the shop, an' goes in, an' I arsts
to be showed a pair of boots. First pair I tried on fitted me
a treat; but I fair rucked that they were too tight for me
corns.

' "Easy, guv'nor," I says, "easy. I want a pair of boots
for walkin' in," I says. "I can't 'ford to sit wiv me trotters
on a sofy smokin' ceegars all day. See?"

'The ole Jew snob says, "Why, they're a splendid fit,"
he says.

' "After you, guv'nor," I replies. "They'd cripple me
'fore I'd walked a dozen yards.'

' "You talk sense," he says. "An' don't your fren want a pair too?" he says.

' "I don't say I won't look at a pair, now you mentioned it," says Maggots. "On'y, don't you clamp up my trotters like what you 'ave my fren's," he says.

' "I'll do you bofe a good turn," says the Jew snob. An' wiv that 'e brings out anuvver pair of boots, an' Maggots tries 'em on. "There," says the ole Jew, "I never in all me life see such fits."

' "Fits it is," says Maggots. "Why, I couldn't 'obble in 'em, let alone walkin'."

'An' wiv that 'e makes a show of 'obblin 'cross the floor of the shop, an' me after 'im, makin' out as if I couldn't 'ardly put one foot down 'fore the uvver. An' soon as we come to the door, Maggots flings it open an' scoots, an' me after 'im. Pace we went was a testermonial to the ole Jew's boots, wiv no error. I like to fink 'ow we got a bit of our own back off that bleed'n' ole Jew.'

Young Alf kicked the toes of his boots viciously against the parapet of the bridge. Then he turned again suddenly to me, and his eyes gleamed, while his mouth worked convulsively.

'I'll see meself righted, if I do five years for it,' he said.

Young Alf then proceeded to explain to me that the small shopkeeper simply invites depredation, by keeping the till just under the counter where any boy can get his hooks on it. This is especially foolish in the case of a shop kept by a woman. It is in such shops that three-fourths of the till-robberies are brought off. A foggy day, a till within easy reach of the first comer, an unprotected woman behind the counter – well, she has only herself to blame if she is robbed.

As an illustration of the folly to which a woman shopkeeper will stoop, young Alf recounted to me his last exploit in the till-lifting line. It was at Peckham. The day was cold, wet, and foggy. And young Alf was going round with a piano-organ, which was wheeled by one of the lads that worked with him. Young Alf finds that a piano-organ gives excellent cover, and enables a boy to see the world without incurring the world's suspicion.

He had ground out a couple of tunes in front of a small shop which dealt in sweets and newspapers, when the woman came out and gave him twopence. Moreover, seeing that his clothes were thin and poor, she said it was a shame that a boy should face such weather without a decent coat to his back. Young Alf was invited into the shelter of the shop, while the kind-hearted woman went upstairs to fetch a coat which had belonged to her son. She had no longer a son to wear it; so she told young Alf.

Young Alf stood alone in the little shop, amazed at the folly of the woman who had left him there. He leaned over the counter and slid the till out.

About fifteen shillings!

He had the choice of fifteen shillings and a few odd coppers, or a second-hand coat which might be worth a good deal less, and was certainly not worth more than that sum. Such was the problem that presented itself to our young friend, nor do I think it was complicated by any other data.

He chose the fifteen shillings – with the odd coppers, and scooted, leaving the other lad to find his way home with the organ.

Once, as young Alf told me this story, I fancied I detected a touch of shame, a mere hint of an apology, in his tone. But I was mistaken.

When he had ended, I hinted that it would have been at least courteous to await the return of the good-hearted woman.

Young Alf saw my meaning; for he is sharp-witted enough.

He explained that when a boy gets hanked by soft-heartedness he is better off the business.

After all, this is a very sound commercial maxim, and lies at the root of bigger businesses than till-snatching.

Anyhow, you will admit that there are a lot of things to be picked up by the boy who can take things as he finds them.

13
Playing for the Pocket

It is not to be supposed that young Alf, having successfully nicked a purse in a fog outside Waterloo Station, as
I have already related, did not follow up a branch of
his profession which promised large profits and quick
returns.

We were making our way together to the pleasant room
of which I have spoken before. It was a dark night, and
especially dark in the small streets which run behind the
place where the Archbishop of Canterbury gives garden-
parties.

'Supposing you wanted to pick my pocket, how would
you set to work?' I asked young Alf.

The question produced a most disconcerting answer.

I had not walked two paces farther when young Alf had
me helpless. He had seized the lapels of my unbuttoned
overcoat, one in either hand, and with a swift jerk pushed
the garment back as far as my elbows. My arms were
pinioned.

'That's one way,' said young Alf, as his eyes gleamed in
my face.

'But I could kick,' I said.

'Not 'fore I'd got yer ticker.'

'But I should chase you.'

'You wouldn't see me. I should be be'ind, an' me pal'd
go froo the pockets.'

'But you haven't got a pal.'

'I shouldn't work wivout a pal, p'r'aps two, where there
wasn't a crowd,' said young Alf, releasing my arms.

I shuffled back into my coat.

'Quarter to ten,' said young Alf, looking at something in his hand, as we came under a lamp-post.

I stopped short.

'I got the ticker,' said young Alf, handing it back to me. His cheeks were puffing convulsively. He was mightily amused.

Replacing the watch in my pocket – though my claim to its possession seemed a poor one – I buttoned up my coat, and walked on, somewhat crestfallen.

'It seems very simple,' I said presently, as we proceeded along the gloomy street. 'But it takes two to do it properly?'

'Free's best,' said young Alf, politely ignoring the success of one. 'Say you was comin' along 'ere, you bein' alone.'

We stood where the street twists into Hercules Buildings, runs into Church Street and the Lambeth Road, and plunges into the limbo beyond.

'Me an' my two pals comes along that way,' continued young Alf, jerking his head towards the Buildings, 'an' one of us steps up an' says, "Got a light, guv'nor". Say it's me. See? Well, as you're feelin' in your pocket an' lookin' at me, anuvver boy whips your coat back, an' the uvver runs froo your pockets. See?'

'But,' I said, 'I could see the boy that went through my pockets, and follow him up.'

Young Alf spat contemptuously.

'Don't you unnerstand?' he said. 'I got you tight all the time, like what I 'ad jest now. The boy what you see runs froo your pockets an' passes the stuff to anuvver boy, an' then they scoot different ways. An' then I drops your coat an' does a scoot anuvver way. See? 'Cause, you unnerstand, we don't get to work 'cept there's more'n one way we can scoot.'

'Then you don't work alone at pocket-picking,' I said.

'Sometimes I done it,' said young Alf. 'Like the time I

told you, outside Waterloo Station. Well not a week ago
nor more there was a toff in the bar at the "Feavers," an' I
see 'im put 'is change into the little pocket side of his coat.
Full up to the knocker, 'e was; an' I see where 'e put 'is
change, you unnerstand. So when 'e goes out, I nips after
'im. Outside there was a bit of a crowd – man sellin'
beeloons – corner of Paradise Street, you know; and I
tumbled against the toff, accidental, an' ketched 'im round
the waist.

' "Beggin' your pardon, guv'nor, for fallin'",' I says.

' "Granted, I'm sure," he says.

'An' 'fore we parted I'd got me 'ooks on to a tanner an'
a couple of browns. Most pelite, 'e was.

'There's anuvver way – wiv a sack,' continued young
Alf presently. 'One boy can work that, if 'e's got the street
to 'imself; on'y two's better. You just drop a sack over the
'ead of a toff, comin' up be'ind him, an' pull it down over
'is shoulders an' as far as 'is knees, an' you can tip 'im up
an' run froo 'im proper. 'Fore he can get out of the sack
you're round the corner. See?'

But on the whole it is better to work with one or two,
or even three or four other boys. So young Alf explained
to me over his ginger-beer and cigar, when we reached the
pleasant room. The risk is distributed.

Besides, the presence of a crowd is favourable to the
operations of a pick-pocket, and the more excited the crowd
is, the greater are the chances of profit. So, when matters
are quiet, it is the business of two of the party to gather a
crowd and keep it interested. The simplest and commonest
method is to get up a fight – a fight that is faked and
friendly, be it understood, but with all the outward sem-
blance of bitter animosity. No unnecessary punishment is
inflicted, though, of course, appearances must be kept up.
Nothing collects a crowd so quickly as a fight, and few
things interest it more. So while the ring of spectators

cheer and hoot the two lads who are rolling over one another in the gutter, two more are hovering to and fro, one of them getting his hooks on to such things as may be hooked, while the other receives and pockets them as quickly as they can be passed. It is most important to remember that no stolen article should be retained about your person an instant longer than is absolutely necessary. On one occasion, young Alf was compelled to keep the result and evidence of his misdeed for two hours in his pocket before planting it, or even passing it. But that was his record. He is not proud of it, regarding it as an error of judgement.

Working one day on the skirts of a crowd which was watching a street-fight – a faked fight – young Alf was lucky enough to have a very smart lad associated with him, a lad who was never more than two feet from his elbow. Now young Alf, by an act of almost criminal folly, permitted an old lady to become aware of the abstraction of her purse. She at once accused him; he was seized by a bystander, and handed over to the police, protesting.

At the station he was searched. No property of any kind whatever was found in his pockets. So he was discharged, to the consternation of the old lady. Young Alf is generous enough to give most of the credit for this escape to the boy who was working with him, and speaks in the highest terms of his admirable backing up.

Working alone is very risky – unless, of course, you are in the dark with a drunken victim – though it is sometimes hard to resist the temptation of a chance opening. But purse-snatching should never be attempted by a boy who does not know the district he is working in and cannot outrun any probable pursuer.

Young Alf has a vivid remembrance of an occasion on which his turn of speed served him well. Only this, with a little ready wit, brought him out of a very tight place.

He was strolling in the city, and looking for any stray articles that could be picked up. Walking down Leadenhall Street, in the direction of Aldgate, he noticed a lady who was looking in at a shop-window. In her hand was a purse which took young Alf's eye.

He snatched it, and ran off at full speed.

'Stop thief!' shrieked the lady.

Several other people took up the cry; and a toff, who nearly succeeded in heading him off, followed close at his heels.

It was an exciting race, for the toff could run a bit. However, young Alf headed eastwards, and felt he was gaining. By this time, the crowd behind him had gained in numbers and in shouting power, and as he turned a corner at Aldgate he noticed that something like a hundred pursuers intervened between him and the toff.

Now there is this curious feature about the crowd that takes part in a man-hunt: most of the pursuers do not know whom they are chasing or why they are chasing him. For the new-comers join in at the front of the mob instead of at the rear, where those who are likely to know most about the matter are falling behind. Moreover, even if the original pursuer can spring decently, he soon finds his path blocked by a mob of excited and useless runners.

Young Alf thinks quickly in an emergency, and this was an emergency to stimulate the most sluggish intelligence. The peculiar characteristic of the crowd that chases a pick-pocket flashed across his mind as he turned the corner at Aldgate, and he concluded that since he could no longer see the toff the toff could no longer see him.

'Stop him!' cried the crowd behind him, and, as they swept along, others stood ready to join in the pursuit.

Young Alf shouted with the crowd.

'Stop 'im! Stop 'im!' he yelled, waving his arms in invitation to the waverers.

'Stop 'oo?' said one and another, attracted by young Alf's excitement, and joining him as he ran.

''Im,' said young Alf. 'Jest turned the corner. I'm blowed, I am. Can't go much furver.'

The crowd swept on, gradually engulfing young Alf.

By this time he had reached a country that he knew. A city of refuge was at hand. There is nothing like a public-house with an entrance in one street and an exit in another.

Young Alf slipped in, nodded to the landlord, and emerged into a quiet street, while the shouts of the crowd pursuing a phantasmal quarry died away in the distance.

Purse-snatching, you will perceive, has its risks. You require special gifts for the pursuit.

Before we parted that evening young Alf told me several more stories of illicit processes. One of them interested me particularly, because it concerned one of the very few cases in which he was aided by a female accomplice. It was a mere ordinary case of theft. But young Alf seemed to enjoy the story. So it shall be given in his own words.

'Lots of toffs bring their own loss on theirselves. It's their own fault, an' their own loss, as you might say. Like the bloke in the bar that was boasting of the brass 'e'd got. Seem to see 'im in me mind's eye now, I do; wiv 'is coat cut smart an' 'is 'at side of 'is 'ead. Gawd! Give me the fair 'ump, it did, hearin' 'im talk. An' I says to meself, "Brass!" I says. "Let's see some of yer brass. Let's 'andle it," I says to meself.'

Young Alf rolled from left to right in his chair as he dug his hands, right and left, into his trouser pockets, which are, as you know, slung high.

'It was in a pub down Battersea,' he continued, 'an' there was more'n one or two of the boys there at the time an' they'll bear me out. Well, presently I sits down beside the toff an' calls him a rare toff an' a lot of old swank of

that kind. Then I give the wheeze to a smart-lookin'
woman there – Lizzie, we called 'er.'

'You knew her?' I asked.

'I hadn't 'ad dealin's wiv 'er, not to speak of,' said young
Alf. 'On'y I knew she was straight, 'cause she was workin'
wiv a pal of mine. See? So Lizzie come over an' I intro-
juiced 'er to the toff as my wife, an' I says—

'"The gen'l'man will make room for you, Lizzie," I
says.

'An' wiv that he made room for Lizzie on the uvver side
from what I was sittin', an' she started larkin' wiv 'im, you
unnerstand. Well, sharp as I knew 'ow I goes froo his left
'and pockets wivout gettin' anyfink worf havin'. Then I
wanted to get to the uvver side. So I told Lizzie she was in
love wiv the toff, 'cause 'e was better-lookin' than what I
was, and I says I was going to take 'er place side of my
'andsome rival. An' wiv that I went an' sat down right side
of the toff.

'Course 'e eggsplained that 'e 'adn't meant no offence,
'aving treated my wife like a lidy; but I made as if I wasn't
easy in me mind. An' there was Lizzie stannin' up front of
'im an' chaffin' an' tellin' 'im not to mind me, bein' only
'cause I was so fond of her, an' me goin' careful froo the
right 'and pockets. See? Well, it 'curred to me that what
brass he'd got was inside his coat, an' I says to meself I
must 'ave that coat wevver or no. So I says to Lizzie I'd
like a coat like that.

'"How you fink," I says, "how you fink I'd look in a
coat like that?"

'"How can I tell wivout I see you wiv one on?" says
Lizzie.

'"That'd be a sight too big for me," I says, looking at
the toff's coat. "The gen'l'man's broader 'cross the chest
than what I am."

'"Not me," he says. He wanted to get back into my

good graces. See? "I bet you drinks," he says, "you fill it as well as I do."

'An' wiv that 'e off with the coat an' I put it on; 'im 'elpin'.

' "What you fink of that?" I says, walkin' up an' down the bar.

' "It's a mile too big," says Lizzie. "Shouldn't 'ardly know you was there."

' "Well, I ain't there," I says, comin' to the door and doin' a scoot.'

Young Alf's cheeks denoted intense amusement at this sally.

''Cause I was somewhere else,' he explained, on recovering his power of speech. 'An' one or two days afterwards there was a rare old liquor up at that pub wiv some of the boys that'd watched the performance. Lizzie come in for 'er share, too. Matter o' ten pounds there was in the inside pocket.'

Young Alf sat with legs extended, his hands in his trouser pockets, and sighed at the recollection.

'And – and about Lizzie—' I said.

14

Lambeth Lasses

Lizzie, it seemed, was an exception and not the rule, being a young woman to whom vice was a living and crime an occasional recreation. She was, as we have seen, useful to young Alf; but young Alf does not speak of her with approval, nor does he admit that she is a typical representative of the Lambeth lass.

In the conversation which followed upon my question concerning Lizzie, young Alf touched upon the sex problem as it presents itself to the Hooligan. It is rather a pity that this conversation cannot be set forth verbatim; for young Alf would appear therein as a chivalrous defender of his womenfolk, and I am conscious that his character, as exhibited in word and deed, requires to be touched up with some highlights before it can be considered a pretty picture.

The average Lambeth lass, as young Alf avers, is neither a prostitute nor a criminal. The former class is regarded with disfavour by young Alf and his friends; for when the toff has been picked clean by the female thief there is very little left for the Lambeth lad. One may honour young Alf's sentiments if one overlooks their origin.

Woman, in Lambeth Walk, as elsewhere, throws her influence into the right scale. She earns her living by hard work in the factories where they make pickles, jam, or mineral waters. Sometimes, too, she sells flowers in the streets. She associates with criminals; but her share in crime is a passive one. Doubtless she suspects that the young man who takes her to the Canterbury, and regales her on sausages and mashed afterwards, is more slippy

with his hooks than behoves an honest lad. But she does
not know or trouble her head about the sort of jobs in
which he is engaged, though, on the whole, she would
rather he went straight than sideways. And if by chance
she is compelled to choose between the law and the lover,
she may be forgiven if she plumps for the lover. She is not,
if we must speak with absolute strictness, virtuous. But
she is rather virtuous, if you will admit degrees in feminine
virtue. She is loyal, strong, and courageous, possessing all
the virtues but virtue. Rough and coarse, if you please,
and foul of tongue when the fit seizes her; but we may call
the roughness honesty, and the foulness slang, without
being far wrong.

They fight, too, on occasion; and young Alf speaks in the
highest terms of the prowess they display. For their fighting is not confined to the scratching of faces, the pulling of
hair, and the mauling of clothes, but consists of dodging,
feinting, countering, and good straightforward hitting,
with muscles hardened by work that would tax the strength
of an ordinary man.

'More'n 'arf the time it's jealousy what leads to scrappin',' said young Alf. 'Say there's two or free gals messin'
about after the same boy; well, they 'ave a set to so's to
settle which is goin' to 'ave 'im. See? On'y sometimes it
comes out the uvver way, same as it did wiv Maggots.'

'What happened to Maggots?' I asked.

'Why, Maggots was walkin' wiv more'n one gal, – more'n
two or free, if it comes to that, and 'e fort it was about time
to make some change. Getting a bit too fick for Maggots, it
was, specially as it'd come to 'is knowledge that some of
the gals'd been fighting to see which of 'em should 'ave
'im. Well, one afternoon one of the gals says to Maggots
that she'd be down the Arches after she'd 'ad 'er tea.
Maggots 'e'd 'ad enough of the gal, so it came into his 'ead
that 'e'd 'ave a bit of a game wiv 'er. So he says 'e'd be

down the Arches after tea, too. Then he nips round an'
makes a 'pointment wiv one gal after anuvver to be down
the Arches after tea, an' they all promised they'd come.'

'And they all came?'

'Eight of 'em, one after the uvver. An' as each one come
the uvvers arst 'er who she'd come to meet, an' she says
Maggots. An' there was all of 'em stannin' down the Arches
waitin' for the same boy. See? 'Course that was jest what
Maggots wanted, 'cause 'e fort there'd be a rare old beano,
'cause all the gals'd been messin' about after 'im.'

'And was there a fight?'

'It didn't turn out quite like Maggots expected; but
there was a fight, in a way of speaking, an' Maggots see it
all, wiv no error. Silly like, 'e goes down to the Arches quiet
as 'e could, finkin' 'e'd like to see the gals an' if they'd
come to meet 'im an' wevver they was scrappin'. See?
On'y the gals they'd been layin' their 'eads togevver, an'
seein' as Maggots'd been playin' a game wiv 'em, they
'greed they'd give Maggots what for. An' soon as Maggots
showed 'is chivvy one of the gals says, "Fink we're Mor-
mons?" she says; an' wiv that she lands him one; an'
quicker'n anyfink the 'ole lot chips in back an' front an'
dusts 'im over proper. Oh! 'e see a fight, Maggots did, that
evenin', but it wasn't the sort of fight that 'e'd set out to
see. They could put in a bit o' work too, them gals could,
'cause Maggots always fancied big gals. Sort of 'obby of
'is. An' 'fore they'd done wiv 'im Maggots wished 'e was
safe at Wormwood Scrubs. See? Nor I don't think any
Lambeth boy'll play on the ikey like that wiv them gals
again.'

Young Alf leaned back and spat straight in front of him.
His lower jaw worked rapidly.

'Then Lizzie belonged to a different class?' I said.

Young Alf crossed one foot over the other and wagged
his head.

'If you come across Lizzie an' she offered you a rose,' he said, 'an' arst you to smell it, it wouldn't be worf your while.'

'Why not?' I asked.

'Fiddled,' said young Alf.

'You mean—'

'Drugged, you unnerstand. You smell the rose, an' in 'arf a mo you dunno anyfink more. See?'

Young Alf dived into an inner pocket, and brought out something which he held in the palm of his hand.

'What you fink of that for a ceegar?' he said.

I took it from him, fingered it, smelt it.

'I don't see anything curious about it,' I said. 'It seems to be an ordinary twopenny smoke. Cabbage, with a bit of tobacco-leaf wrapped round. Eh?'

''Tain't,' said young Alf. 'Not be a long chalk. Like to smoke it, jest a little bit of it?'

'I think I'd prefer one of my own,' I replied.

'You're about right,' said young Alf. 'It's a faked ceegar.'

'Drugged?'

Young Alf nodded, and returning the cigar carefully to his inner pocket, he leaned forward and dropped his voice to a hoarse whisper. 'There's been a lot o' talk about druggin' liquor in pubs, puttin' snuff in, y' know. Well, even if you got a mug that you fink you can skin easy, it ain't so easy to fiddle 'is drink in a bar where there's lots of uvver people; you can take it from me. It ain't the drink that gets fiddled. The way a mug gets struck senseless is be ceegars. And cigarettes. See?'

Young Alf sat back and regarded me obliquely.

'It wasn't on'y a week ago,' he continued, 'I come across a toff in a bar that was 'avin' a bit extry, an' gettin' extry good-natured wiv it. So course I got into conversation wiv 'im, an' 'e stood drinks. Wasn't boozed, 'e wasn't, an' I reckon 'e was pretty fly, 'cause 'e kep' 'is coat buttoned tight. On'y he was talkin' free about the brass 'e'd got. Says 'e could buy up the 'ole bar an' all the bleed'n' crowd in it. Well, I finks I must run froo 'im if I see me way, on'y I couldn't see no pals stannin' around, an' I couldn't see me way until sudden like it come into me 'ead 'ow to work the job. An' me wiv me ceegar in me pocket all the time! See?

'Well, presently I brings out me ceegar an' offers it to him, be way of returnin' the compliment of the drink 'e'd stood. See? An' course 'e takes it an' lights up.

' "That's a nice smoke," 'e says.

' "Oughter be," I chips in. "It come a long way 'fore it got 'ere. You don't get a smoke like that every day of the week, an' countin' Sundays," I says. An' that was Gawd's trewth.'

The contortion of young Alf's face denoted intense amusement.

'Well, 'fore long,' continued young Alf, 'the toff began to get queer in 'is 'ead. 'Cause, you unnerstand, it was a faked ceegar what I'd give 'im. So I looks round at the uvver people in the bar, an' I says that my fren's a bit overcome an' I fink I'll take 'im into the fresh air. See? An' wiv that out we goes togevver, me tellin' 'im 'ow the fresh air'll liven 'im up like. An' time I'd got a 'ansom an' put 'im inside, the job was worked. Went froo 'im, carm an' easy, I did, while we drove along. An' then, soon as we come to a pub that I knew was awright, I stopped the cab an' says I was goin' to get some brandy for my fren' that wasn't feelin' well. 'Course I nips froo an' out at the back.'

'And what happened to the man in the cab, and the cabman?' I asked.

'Never see eiver of 'em again,' said young Alf. 'Don't want to.'

'Let me see that cigar again,' I said.

He drew it out with great care, and handed it to me.

'I rather fancy I detect a curious perfume about it,' I said. 'Not very marked, but still—'

'Not if you was a bit boozed,' said young Alf.

'Where do you buy those cigars?' I asked.

Young Alf returned the cigar to his pocket, puffed his cheeks once, but said nothing.

There are some things that young Alf will not tell me. He will not tell me where you get drugged cigars. But he knows where they are to be bought, and he knows what you must ask for when you want them.

'What you got to be careful of,' said young Alf as we were parting, 'is flahers, an' ceegars. An' cigarettes,' he added, as he turned at the door.

15
Politics

Young Alf was late for his appointment. We had arranged
to meet on the Embankment in the neighbourhood of
Cleopatra's Needle, at eleven; and the quarter past had
just boomed from Westminster. It was a clear night, with
a full moon shining and turning the Thames into a fairy
river spanned by bridges of gossamer. Have you never
seen Charing Cross railway bridge by moonlight? As I
came up in the train I encountered a party of people who
were going out to see the illuminations, for it was the
Prince of Wales' birthday. Why do people not go out in
parties to lean over the parapet of the Embankment and
watch the Thames by moonlight? The river always has its
fascination. On a dark night, when the drizzle drenches to
the skin, and the Embankment is empty of its customary
tenants, the river is mysterious, and a little bit awful.
Awful, because you can see nothing of it. Only an occasional flicker of light through the rain. You hear the puff
of engines, which cross the sky and now and then stop to
whistle impatiently. Now and again the throb of a passing
tug, which, unseen, steals out of hearing. Below you, the
lap of the water against the concrete – the wash from the
stern of the tug. You lean over, and look into blackness.
You think of despairing women who cast themselves over
bridges into the outstretched arms of death. A boat creeps
into hearing; there are pauses between the strokes, as
though the rower were given to meditation. The river-
police. Yes; it is the Styx, and here is Charon.

But this evening it was fairyland. The tide was at the
full, and the moonlight transfigured the sordid details of

the Surrey side. Fairyland in front, as you leaned over the parapet and watched the silver path of the moon upon the river break into ten million diamonds as the tug crossed it. But turn, and you are facing the Inferno.

In the distance, somewhere, someone is playing a tune on a penny whistle:

> 'Oh! Come all ye Faithful,
> Joyful and triumphant!'

– An enterprising musician, with a sense of the fitness of things; for we are near the season of Advent, when our mood demands that hymn. Here comes one of them, too. Neither joyful nor triumphant, but shuffling along upon a leg that is manifestly inadequate to its task. He stops now and then; and then he comes on. You could have told him, having walked along from Charing Cross. The seats are full. He must be new to misery if he expects to find an empty seat on the Embankment after eleven at night, and not a cold night. Why, already there are some, less lucky than the rest, sleeping on the pavement, their backs propped against the parapet.

He passes on, and I see no more of him. No doubt there is plenty of room in Trafalgar Square, or if that by any chance is full, Hyde Park is a spacious bedroom.

Save for an occasional cab the Embankment is very quiet. Now and then an arm is flung, or a dim form shifts with a grunt into an easier position. But, on the whole, it is an abode of silence. Early rising is the rule among those who sleep on the Embankment, and that renders it advisable to go to sleep as early as possible. The lap-lap of the river against the Embankment wall was a sort of lullaby.

And here is young Alf, coming noiselessly along from the direction of the Temple Station. His walk is quite unmistakable, – a slouch that is in no way akin to feebleness.

We exchange greetings; young Alf's mode of greeting does not extend beyond an announcement of his own presence. And I at once noticed a tinge of depression in his aspect.

Young Alf is never merry; as you have already heard, he is not addicted to laughter; nor can I conceive him uplifting his voice in song. On the other hand, he is by no means melancholic. His temperament is equable, and he accepts good and evil fortune as coming from the same unknown source over which he, personally, has no control. Hitherto I had not seen him elated, nor had I seen him cast down. But this evening there was certainly a note of depression in his voice as well as in his deportment.

We leaned over the parapet in silence for a few moments. Then young Alf said:

'They bin tryin' to get 'old o' me.'

'Who?' I inquired.

'The Awmy,' he replied.

'A very good thing, too,' I said. 'Why don't you enlist? It's a fine healthy life.'

'I dessay,' said young Alf; 'there's more'n one of my pals gone for a sojer. On'y I didn't mean that. I meant the Salvation Awmy. See? They bin tryin' to get 'old o' me.'

'Well?'

'Bin into the place where I kip last free nights, the bloke 'as. Wants me to join the Awmy! "Come to Jesus! Come to Jesus." You know what they say. Got a light? I eggspect they want to carry me round, – sort o' show-like – converted 'Ooligan – eh?'

Young Alf lighted the stump of a cigarette with the match I gave him.

'Well, anyway,' I said, 'I expect they would put you in the way of earning an honest living.'

Young Alf shrugged his shoulders contemptuously.

'That's all very well for some,' he said. 'But it ain't good enough for a boy that's up to 'is graft. Not be a long chalk.'

There was silence for a few moments, while young Alf puffed at his cigarette. Then he dropped it in the shadow over the parapet, and I heard the ghost of a fizz in the water below.

'There's plenty of dust-'ole lurchers that make out they're class,' he continued, 'an' never did nuffink long as they lived to show 'eart. And I dessay they might be got round easy for a pork pie or a night's doss. But they ain't the boys that work the biz down the Walk; don't you make no meestike. The boy that done a bit o' class don't want for somefink to fill 'is mouf wiv. 'Course, if it's a evenin's beano, wiv a supper frown into the show – why, I've bin meself, jest as a bit of old swank. But you don't ketch me takin' on the sort o' job the Awmy puts in yer way. Bit o' food an' a night's doss, an' work 'ard for it too.'

Young Alf spat viciously into the Thames.

'They don't give yer a chawnce,' he said, gloomily.

'But,' I objected, 'I'm always hearing of Associations, and Societies, and Leagues, and so on, which aim at raising the – I mean they aim at giving you a chance. Why, there are young men who come from Oxford and Cambridge and live in settlements in the lowest quarters of London in order to – well – in order to give you a—'

'I know all about that,' said young Alf. 'There's toffs come down Lambef way, an' I've showed 'em round. One night two of 'em come an' arst me an' Maggots to show 'em round. Show 'em everyfink, they said. One of 'em was a orfer.'

'A – what?'

'Orfer, wrote about fings in the papers.'

'Ah, of course.'

'So me an' Maggots walked round wiv 'em, an' showed

116

'em where the fences lived, an' one or two uvver fings, you
unnerstand. An' then they wanted to see some more,
wanted to see where I kipped, if *you* please. So I fort it was
time to pull down their ear. Wasn't likely we'd get much
if we waited till the show was over. See? So I says there
was a doss close by, an' what was they goin' to spring.
Well, we couldn't pull down their ear for more'n 'arf a
dollar. An' soon as we got that we nipped on to a tram
and left 'em. No. They 'adn't seen nuffink. What you
fink?'

'Well, I expect they were rather disappointed,' I said.

'Fort they was goin' to see 'orrors,' continued young Alf,
'an' they didn't see nuffink. I know that sort. Come down
jest as if they was goin' to look at a lot o' wild beasties. I sin
'em, too, when a lot o' prisoners was bein' took from one
jug to anuvver. Starin' at 'em, – somefink cruel. I bin
there meself. Why can't they take the prisoners early in
the mornin' when there ain't no one about; or else late at
night when no one can't see 'em? Eh? They don't give us a
chawnce. Not a 'arf chawnce.'

Young Alf's eyes gleamed rather savagely, and he spoke
as though he meant what he was saying. I seemed to have
struck a deeper layer of his nature.

'What'd be the good o' me tryin' to go straight?' asked
young Alf. 'Fink they'd let me? not them.'

Young Alf leaned over the parapet, and picked viciously
at the stonework.

The half-hour boomed out from Westminster, and I
turned in the direction of the sound. The electric light was
gleaming from the summit of the clock-tower, indicating
that our law-makers were still at work.

'Now, I wonder what the devil they're talking about,'
I said.

'Eh?' said young Alf, looking round at me suspiciously.

'In the House – the House of Commons,' I said. 'That's

the House of Commons, where they make the laws under which you and I live.'

'Needn't tell me that,' said young Alf; 'I sin it often enough.'

'But, Alf, don't you realize?' I said; for the absurdity of things in general had caught hold upon me, and I was myself absurd. 'Don't you realize that that electric light blazes over seven hundred men, who are pledged to make this country a pleasant place for you and me to dwell in? Don't you realize that men have been sitting for hundreds of years in that place, trying to make us honest and respectable? Don't you realize that the very object of the British Constitution, from the ballot-box up to the electric light on the top of the clock-tower, is to make the world comfortable for everyone who leads an honest life. And young Alf, why aren't you honest?'

Young Alf shifted round and faced me.

'What's the use o' talkin'?' he said.

'It's a big place,' I continued, looking up the river at the Houses of Parliament, with their rows of lighted windows and the little button of electric light on top. 'Inside, seven hundred of the finest men in Great Britain. Behind them, the civil service, the police, and the British Army and Navy – all bent on making you a good boy. It's long odds, young Alf. Then there's the Church, too; with the archbishops and the clergy of the diocese, curates, and all; to say nothing of ministers of all denominations, district visitors and philanthropists. Vestries, too, and Parish Councils, and – Lord, yes! – the London County Council. The Lord Chamberlain and the Censor of Plays as well; the Lord Mayor and Aldermen, and the Common Councillors, and the Judges of first instance, and the Judges of— Good gracious me! young Alf! All this mass of authority against nine stone something of lawlessness. You can't fight it, young Alf. Parliament, police, Judges, Army, Navy, and

Reserve Forces, with Her Majesty the Queen at the summit,
– you had better step over to the other side and shout with
the bigger crowd, young Alf.'

'What's the use o' talkin'?' said young Alf again.

I looked around at him. His teeth were set hard.

'Doesn't that impress you?' I asked, nodding in the
direction of our Legislature.

He stared moodily at it for a few moments.

'What I can't make out is what they call pol'tics,' he
said. 'First it's one side, an' then it's the uvver side; an'
when all's said an' done, where's the good of it, eh? Why,
when there's a 'lection on, there's toffs an' ladies down our
way, fick as beetles. Fair worry Jimmy off 'is rocker, they
do, wantin' 'im to vote. An' when the 'lection's over an'
one side or the uvver's got in over there, why, nuffink
comes of it. There's 'nough cops an' splits in Lunnun to
eat up the 'Ooligans for their breakfast. Don't you tell me.
Parlymint ain't no bleed'n' good.'

'It can put you in gaol, Alf,' I said.

'It's put me gaol more 'n once,' said young Alf. 'An' fat
lot o' good it done me.'

I found it difficult to base an argument in favour of the
prison system on the case of young Alf himself; so I said
nothing.

'Strikes me,' continued young Alf, 'I'd like to get up a
pawty of me own down our way, an' go to Parlymint
meself. I could put 'em up to a quiff or two, wiv no error.'

I asked young Alf what steps he would take to reform
the criminal classes, if he were elected to Parliament and
attained a position of authority. And young Alf's views,
which must be regarded in one sense at least, as the views
of an expert, appeared to me very interesting.

You must catch the criminal young, he maintains; in
fact, before he has become a criminal. Take him as soon as
he begins associating with those who are known to be

going sideways, lift him clean out of his surroundings, and teach him a trade. Make him a sailor, a soldier, teach him carpentry, bricklaying, anything that will give him regular employment and regular pay. But do this before he has had time to taste the sweets of irregular employment and indefinite reward.

Above all, do not send him to gaol.

Do not send him to gaol, even though you catch him rifling your safe in the small hours.

Young Alf does not believe in the efficacy of prison treatment for juvenile offenders.

Certainly, the young Hooligan who has never been in gaol is rather inclined to shrink from the experience. The punishment is still an unknown quantity, and the mystery engenders terror. But after a term of imprisonment, when the gaol is no longer a mystery, and the boy has found that he is subjected to no personal violence, has enough to eat without the necessity of stealing or working for it, and has to endure no particular inconvenience beyond conforming to certain simple rules, – then the gaol loses its terrors, and he is willing to face it again if the need arises. He looks forward to doing a bit of time as the young gentleman in the drapery emporium looks forward to stocktaking, – a nuisance, but all in the day's work, and with a bit of a beano when it is over.

It might be imagined that the mere disgrace of being handcuffed, placed in the dock, sentenced in full view of the public, and carted off in a prison van to do time at Wandsworth, would appeal to the youngster who was hesitating between taking a situation as an errand boy at three and sixpence a week, and working – we will say – with such as Jimmy, – between going straight and going sideways. There are strata in society in which people fight shy of the man who is known to have been convicted of felony and paid the usual penalty. But in the class of which young Alf was speaking this feeling does not exist at all. The boy who has done time is not disgraced in his own circle. On the contrary, he is a bit of a hero in his small way. It is not necessary to get lagged – if you are known to have shown heart. But if you have been lagged, sent to the stir, and done time, – well – that is pretty good proof that you are class.

That is why young Alf, though proud of the fact that he has never done a stretch for burglary, is not by any means sorry to have spent some two years of his short life behind the bars. He is thereby put above suspicion.

Young Alf, then, would not send the youthful malefactor to prison. He would catch him, at the first sign of stumbling, and send him to a reformatory school, there to learn some honest trade that will hereafter keep him in comfort and out of mischief. He holds that if Parliament went the right way to work, a good many of the youngsters who are getting into the ranks of the Hooligans might be pointed for the straight and narrow way.

It would be an odd experiment, I reflected, as I looked from young Alf to the Mother of Parliaments, to organize a Select Committee, with young Alf as chairman, charged to find the best means of reforming the Hooligan. Not so absurd, after all. For young Alf knows as much about the question as most people.

The light on the clock-tower was extinguished. 'There!' I said. 'The sitting is over. I wonder what they have been doing tonight.'

'Oh, Parlymint's no good,' said young Alf. 'That's what Jimmy's always said. You got to look after yerself. No one else won't. They don't give us a chawnce.'

In the distance a violin squeaked 'The Mistletoe Bough.' The penny whistle still persevered with 'O come, all ye Faithful!' though from the sound I gathered that it had moved on to the next licensed premises.

'You get pinched, an' you do yer bit o' time, an' you come out, an' you get pinched again; that's what it is. Same ole game. Gimme a chawnce. I'd talk to 'em. Fings I could tell 'em. Don't you talk to me 'bout pol'tics. Finkin' about themselves all the time; that's what they're doin'. See?'

'Then, what is your feeling about going to gaol?' I asked. 'Don't you mind it?'

Young Alf considered a bit.

Then he confessed that, on the whole, he didn't. Prison life he did not regard as at all unendurable. When you have taken the plunge it doesn't really hurt. Sometimes you come across a warder who is a bit of a hot 'un, and then you suffer for it. But, taking one thing with another, you might be in a worse place than Wandsworth gaol, – or even Wormwood Scrubs; a good deal depends upon the warder. No; on the whole, you don't mind doing time, providing you have done it before, – and not too many times. When you've got a lot of previous convictions against you, and done several stretches, and are getting on in life, you know that the next sentence will probably see you into your grave. Then you decide that it is more profitable to swing than to do another stretch, and you buy a revolver, load it, and on occasion use it.

That was Jimmy's situation just before he succeeded in amassing sufficient capital to start as a respectable fence.

'But is that game worth the candle?' I asked. 'Why not turn it up and live an honest life. That's just what gaol is meant for, – to persuade you that it's more comfortable to go straight than sideways.'

'It's no good when you once got lagged,' said young Alf. 'They don't give you a chawnce again. What you fink a boy's goin' to do when he comes out. Eh? You fink they give 'im a job? Not them.'

'But what about this prison-gate mission?' I said. 'I

always understood that when a prisoner came out of gaol, he was met at the gates, taken to have breakfast, and offered a chance of living an honest life.'

Then young Alf gave his opinion of the prison home which well-meaning philanthropists offer to the discharged prisoner. I fancy he was prejudiced, and I will not set forth his criticism in detail. But, in effect, his opinion was that there is not enough difference between the prison and the home outside the gates to induce a boy to choose the certainty of the latter rather than the chance of the former. Moreover, if you are not a skilled workman at some trade other than house-breaking or pocket-picking, you won't get wages enough to live on. If you are a skilled workman, you will get less than the ordinary rate of wages, because you are only taken on as a favour, being a discharged prisoner. Oh, no! Politics don't give you a chance.

'But there's always some pals to meet you when you done your time,' continued young Alf. 'You come out in the mornin', feelin' as if all the world was against you, an' there's free or four pals waitin' wiv a word o' welcome. Makes you feel you've got some frens left. See? An' then you 'ear what's bin goin' on, an' if anyfink big's comin' off. See? It's the symperfy.'

Young Alf's hands were dug deep into his pockets, and his shoulders were hunched about his ears.

'There's always pals to meet you,' he said. 'An' they show more symperfy than a toff gives to 'is daughter what's got led crooked.'

The Embankment was quite silent, now that a cab had clattered past and disappeared by the Temple Station.

'But solitary confinement—' I suggested. 'Isn't that rather unpleasant? Doesn't that frighten the prisoner?'

'Sends some of 'em dotty,' replied young Alf. 'But I don't mind it meself. If you in the crib-crackin' line it

gives you a chawnce of finkin' out some job you can put
your 'and to when you come out. You got time enough to
fink, wiv no error.'

'But do you mean to tell me that it's impossible to get
an honest job when you've come out of gaol?' I asked.

'Can't be done,' said young Alf. 'There's lots o' men
gone in for crackin' cribs jest 'cause they couldn't seport
their famblies. Don't you b'lieve it?'

I didn't – quite.

'Look 'ere, I'll tell yer,' said young Alf. 'I 'ad a honest
job once.'

'When you were tiger to a toff?' I said.

'No, not then. It was a real honest job, strite. I 'ad a
place at a general store, – coals an' grocery, and fings like
that; an' 'fore long I 'ad the management of the 'ole show;
I was as careful of every penny of me master's money as I
was of me own, an' took a dam sight more care of it than
what 'e did. An' then one day there comes a split pokin' 'is
nose into the show. Sin me drivin' round wiv the pony cart.
See? An' 'e tells my master that I done time. Then what
'appened?'

'Well?'

''Course I got the push.'

'That was hard lines.'

'Got a bit o' me own back, though.'

'How was that?'

'I see what was comin'. An' when I took the pony on me
rounds, I taught 'im not to let anybody drive 'im but me.
See? I can always get along wiv anyfink in the shape of a
'awse; an' 'fore I'd done wiv that pony 'e'd do anyfink I
told 'im to. An' no one else couldn't 'andle 'im. I reckon
they 'ad a fair ole time wiv that pony when I got the push.
'Arf killed the master, I unnerstand.'

Young Alf thought he must be going.

'Supposing someone were to offer you a job,' I said.

'I bin finkin',' said young Alf. 'If I could get a job as watchman.'

'Watchman!'

The idea seems ludicrous enough.

'Look 'ere,' he said. 'You know them spy-'oles they 'ave in shops – an' places – so's the copper can look in, eh? well, they ain't no good. 'Cause, if I'm workin' a shop like that, I've got me pal outside, an' when the cop comes along I get the wheeze, an' lay down unnerneath the spy-'ole, so's the cop can't see me. What they want's a man that'll set up all night an' keep a eye on the place. Don't you fink so? You fink I could get a job as watchman?'

It seemed doubtful.

And yet if I were quite sure that young Alf were on my side, I would ask no better guardian against burglars.

Young Alf watched me narrowly.

'That want's a bit o' c'rac'ter, I s'pose,' he said.

'I'm afraid it does, Alf,' I replied.

16

A Bit of an Argument

Young Alf is not, as you will have gathered, a man of peace. He has fought his fellows again and again, with varying success. But there is more than one kind of fighting. You may fight under Queensberry rules, and I have seen young Alf so trammelled, as I shall shortly recount. You may, on the other hand, fight without any rules at all, with the sole object of rendering your opponent incapable of any further action in the immediate future. I have seen young Alf fighting in that way too, and shall not speedily forget it.

But the fight on Barnes Common was, as I understand, just a fair set to with the raws. I did not have the satisfaction of witnessing it. But young Alf related to me the story of the encounter with such evident satisfaction, and such obvious pride in the result, that I think you must hear it as it came from his own lips.

'Toughest fight I ever 'ad in me life,' said young Alf, 'was one Sunnay morning over Barnes Common wiv a dam big lab'rin' chap. I 'adn't no idea of gettin' to close quarters wiv 'im, not when I see 'im in at the "Lamb an' Flag", 'cause I 'adn't 'ardly ever sin 'im afore. On'y we was all talkin' togevver in the bar an' we got into a bit of a argyment over runnin'. See? Well, you know I can do a bit in the runnin' line, else why do my pals call me "The Deer", eh? An' so it warn't more 'n you'd expect that I'd get my monkey up when the lab'rer began makin' sneerin' remarks, an' makin' out 'e didn't fink I could run like what I said I could. So one fing led to anuvver, an' 'fore long the lab'rer sung out that 'e fort 'e could do anyfink that I could.

' "In fightin'?" I ys.

' "I said anyfink, didn't I?" 'e says. "An' what I says I mean." That's how 'e give it back to me.

' "An' when?" I says.

' "When you like an' for what you like, so long as it ain't over a crown." That was the lab'rer's conditions, you unnerstand.

'Wiv that there was a lot of talk 'bout where we should scrap, but 'fore we left the pub it was 'greed we should meet for a go to a finish on Barnes Common at seven o'clock on the next Sunnay morning, promisin' that on'y our own partic'ler pals on each side should be let into the know.

'Well, Sunnay mornin' come, an' there was me a bit before me time at the place on Barnes Common that we'd 'greed upon. The lab'rer come punkshal too, an' there was about a dozen or more pals come down to see the scrap. Soon as the lab'rer began peelin' I see quite plain that I was givin' away a lump in weight. On'y don't you fink I funked the job, 'cause I didn't. See?

'I'd settled in me mind that I'd go a bit light for the first two or free rounds so's I could see what the lab'rer was made of wivout gettin' winded meself. But I soon found I'd got me work cut out if I wanted to stan' up 'gainst him for long. I was quicker 'n what 'e was, but I was givin' 'im two stone an' more. After the first round it didn't look over an' above rosy for your 'umble. Still, there wasn't nuffink broken, nor yet in the second round neiver.

'We 'adn't 'ardly got into the third round 'fore I see I'd got a reg'lar sneezer to 'andle. An' 'bout 'arf way froo I got a flattener on me razzo that pretty nigh laid me out, an' 'fore I knew anyfink more my right eye went in for early closin'. 'Ealfy, wasn't it? Much as I could do to keep stannin' up, that round.

'Well, I settled in me mind that round four was to be my look in if I wasn't to go under, so I went for the lab'rer wiv all me bloody might, an' got in free hot 'uns on 'is ribs that fair made 'is timbers crack, an' 'fore the round was finished I'd landed a couple of stingers on 'is dial that seprised 'im proper.

'The fifth round was 'ammer an' tongs again, an' the lab'rer got one of my teef to give notice, but I got one back on 'is jore, an' there was the lab'rer comin' at me wiv 'is tongue 'angin' right out of 'is mouf. Well, I see me chance then, an' I give 'im a upper cut that made 'im fair bite into 'is tongue an' go down full length on the grass. The next round was the last, an' a little 'oliday for me it was, wiv no error. 'E couldn't 'ardly put up 'is dukes be that time, an' I knocked 'im out first time I smacked 'im.

'I've 'ad a good many scraps in me time, nor it wouldn't seprise me if I was to have some more. But I don't never expect to 'ave a tougher fight than I 'ad that mornin' on Barnes Common. It was 'ard sloggin' all froo; an' if I didn't fair earn me five bob that mornin', – well, I never earned five bob in all me life. Don't you fink so?'

17
Strange Dwellings

Somewhat doubtfully the servant announced that a young
man was waiting in the hall and wished to see me. I bade
her show him up to my study. Half-a-minute later young
Alf came noiselessly up the stairs, hesitated a moment at
the door with a quick glance round the room, and entered.
He had prepared himself carefully for his call. The top
button of his coat, which had been missing for many weeks,
was represented by a substitute. He had shaved. And his
neckerchief – the blue one with the white spots – was
folded with the utmost neatness. He seated himself before
the fire, leaned forward with his elbows on his knees, and
his cap bunched between his hands. I expressed a hope
that he had had no difficulty in finding my house. In reply
he hinted that so far from having any difficulty in finding
the house, he would have had no difficulty in effecting an
entry without the aid of the servant who opened the door.

This led us naturally to the subject of burglary, and I
turned my chair and listened to what my guest had to say.

Young Alf spoke with scorn of the burglar who boasts
of the time he has done. This is no legitimate ground for
boasting. It is as though the fighting man should boast of
being knocked out, or the bookmaker take pride in his
losses. If you are caught you have shown your incompetence. And though young Alf has been pinched once or
twice for minor offences, such as passing snide coin, he has
never done a stretch for burglary.

'I come near it more 'n once, but I never fell,' he said.
'Once I should have fell, on'y I got up the chimbly. I was
workin' a job at a country 'ouse, 'bout fifteen miles out of

129

Lunnun. I fort it was awright, 'cause the famb'ly was away. But I s'pose I must have made more noise than what I oughter 'ave, an' 'earing a sort of rushing about, I made a dash for the chimbly. It was one of them old chimblys – in the 'all – wiv pigeon-holes for the climbin' boys to put their 'ands an' feet, so I could keep up awright while they was wonderin' what it was they'd 'eard. Raver 'ealfy, wasn't it? On'y they never fort of lookin' up the chimbly.'

That was the narrowest squeak that young Alf ever had, in his own opinion. But he is particularly anxious that no one should think the less of him for never having done a stretch for burglary. He argues, quite reasonably, that the perfect burglar is never caught, and consequently never does a stretch. It is to his immunity from arrest that he owes his position as leader of his gang.

I alluded to Charles Peace, who has always appealed to me as the ideal burglar – suave, certain, and secretive. The history of that eminent man, who was well-known in the Walk, is familiar to young Alf. He speaks of Charles Peace with the respect due to the great dead, but is always a little annoyed to hear him cracked up as anything out of the way in the burgling line. The old man, he thinks, would not be much to the front in these days of working jobs in record time. Besides, he was no flyer; and, while young Alf never saw a cop to whom he could not give a good start and a bad beating, there are a good many who could have outspun Peace. But then, as you know, running is one of young Alf's hobbies. To run well and far you must be loose in the girth; and policemen wear belts.

Anyhow, now that you have heard young Alf's argument, you will not, I trust, think any the worse of him for never having done a stretch for burglary.

Young Alf attaches great importance to the planning of a job, and neglects no means of making himself acquainted with the interior arrangements of any house he proposes to visit. There are many ways of gaining this information. The commonest is to set out with a few plumber's tools and offer your services in looking over the cistern and pipes. This method, of course, can only be adopted in the winter. Besides, young Alf considers the fake a little overdone. Nevertheless, it has its advantages; for, while you are pretending to tinker with the cistern, you can not only get a good idea of the position of the various rooms and the best means of effecting an entry, but you are morally certain to be able to pick up any stray articles that seem to want taking care of. Some men favour the insurance book as disarming suspicion, now that so many people have taken to the insurance business. It is easy enough to get hold of an insurance book; and even if you have none it doesn't much matter, as it is scarcely likely that anyone will ask to see it. But the insurance book will not gain you admission to the best houses, such as the really smart burglar wishes to have upon his visiting list. Young Alf thinks that the best dodge is to send one of the gang with flowers or ferns for sale. As soon as the door is opened he puts his eye over the bolts and fastenings, the run of the staircase, and gets a general notion of the plan of the house. The chances are that he will not sell any flowers at the front door. So he wanders round to the servants' premises, noting how the grounds lie, and what entrances are available.

Young Alf does not approve of the rope-ladder which the late Charles Peace used. A better plan is to stand upon the shoulders of your pals. But then it must be remembered that Peace worked without companions. A rope, however, comes in handy when you have to climb high and have a chance to lasso a chimney. You must carry the end up in your teeth in case a copper should notice it hanging down. No burglar-proof window-fastener has yet been invented. For young Alf holds that the best of patents falls before a

diamond fixed in one leg of a pair of compasses, whereby a
circle of any required size may be cut out of the window.
If you gently push the surrounding portion you can pick
out the circular piece with a pair of tweezers, or even with
a pin. Then there is nothing to prevent your unfastening
the catch. Once an entrance is effected, shut the window
behind you. Nothing attracts the suspicion of a policeman
like an open window. But note carefully its position, in
case you have to make a sudden retreat. A burglar prefers
to leave a house unostentatiously by the door. There are,
however, occasions on which decent time is not afforded
for a quiet and respectable exit, and you are compelled to
jump through a window. That requires some doing.
Remember to go through sideways, adopting a sparring
attitude. You will thus save your face, and also avoid
identification. Electric bells under the door-mats and on
the stairs need not worry you, for you will not step on a
mat, but straddle it, and usually only the middle and top
steps are wired. It is safer, however, to go up by the
banisters. Creaking boards are sometimes an annoyance
even to the lightest-footed crib-cracker. Young Alf carries
a set of wedges which shut together like a telescope. He
carries, too, a small supply of oil for the lubrication of any
noisy article of furniture on which he proposes to operate.

Having thus gained entrance, it will be your own fault
if you do not make the best use of your time. Let your
visit be as short as possible, resist the temptation of re-
freshment (you will have taken a nip of brandy before
getting to work on the window), and on no account omit to
look behind the pictures. Young Alf expresses great sur-
prise at the prevalence of this habit of hiding valuables
behind pictures, which are invariably searched by the
experienced burglar. He recommends a safe built into the
wall. Having three of its sides guarded it cannot be played
round; in fact, young Alf holds that a first-class safe of this

kind cannot be tackled in any reasonable time, and without more risk than most men care to incur.

Finally, do not wire the lawn. The wires are of no use unless you have to do a scoot. If you do, you are likely to fall into your own trap, being naturally flustered.

Burglaries are often committed on the information given away by servants, but young Alf thinks the servant is usually quite unaware of the purpose for which the information is required. The young man who walks out with her, and takes a sympathetic interest in her employers' affairs, rarely takes a hand in the actual work. He is known as a 'black cap' or a 'white sheep', and is usually looked upon as useful in his way, but a bit too soft for the hard grind of the business.

There was one occasion, however, on which young Alf secured an accomplice from the inside, a young man in the cashier's department of a big business house; and at this he hinted as he leaned forward in his favourite attitude, elbows upon knees, and his cap rolled into a ball between his palms.

'Time I'm speakin' of, I'd 'ad a bit of luck,' said young Alf. 'There was a job come in me way that brought me a nice little lump of ready, an' I was chuckin' me brass about just like a toff. Looked like a toff, too, I did.'

Young Alf threw himself back in his chair, and thrust his hands into his pockets. 'Wiv me top 'at, all shiny, an' a bleed'n' big stinker in me mouf. What *you* fink, eh?'

I said I should like to hear more about it, and asked what was the nature of the job.

Young Alf was silent for a moment or two. Then he looked at me from the tail of his eye. 'I'd been robbin' a museum,' he said.

'Robbing a museum!' I repeated. 'Where? And what of?'

Young Alf's lower jaw was hard at work; but no answer came. He would not tell me of this exploit. He would only tell me that someone in America – a showman, he thought – wanted a particular object, a specimen of which existed in a museum in England. To young Alf came through various hands a commission to carry off the specimen in question. Young Alf carried out his commission successfully, and had no reason to complain of his reward.

So it happened, that, being flush of brass, young Alf frequented the bars in the neighbourhood of Oxford Street, at the hours when the houses of business closed, and stood drinks, with discrimination, casting his bread, as it were, on the waters, in the hope that it would return as buttered toast.

"Fore long,' said young Alf, 'I'd marked me young man; sawft-'eaded bloke, he was; fort a lot of me. Got quite pals like, we did, meetin' every evenin' be 'pointment at the same ole 'ouse. Course for all me ole swank I didn't say nuffink about bein' on the crooked. See? Least not at first. On'y, one night I remawked I was on for a bit of a game, an' wouldn't he come up to the Oxford wiv me? So we goes along to the Oxford togevver, an' gargled a bit, an' then we looked in at one bar an' annuver, garglin' as per before, an' time it was twelve o'clock, me young man was – 'e was jest 'ow I fort 'e'd be. 'Cause, you unnerstand, I'd settled it all in me mind 'ow I was goin' to work.

'So I says to him, "'Ow'd it be if you was to land a nice little lump on yer own?"

'Well, 'e says 'e could do wiv a bit of ready, on'y 'e didn't see where it was to come from. An' wiv that I rang in me tale, 'ow there was stuff in 'is awfice that 'e could put 'is 'ooks on, an' 'ow I knowed a way to help 'im if he'd stan' in wiv me.

'That skeered 'im, like, at first, an' he said he didn't want to frow away 'is employment.

' "Garn," I says, "there's you at your graft day in an' day out, an' gettin' five-an'-twenty bob a week; an' here's me, livin' like a toff, an' doin' a job 'ere an' a job there, jest as the fancy takes me." See? More'n that, I told 'im he'd 'ave nuffink to do 'cept 'andin me 'is keys.

' "Well, he didn't fall that night, nor the next night. But he fort a lot of 'avin' me for a pal, an' what wiv one fing an' annuver he was gettin' short of ready. Long an' short of it was the job was worked awright.'

'How did you work it?' I said.

The method was simple. Young Alf strolled into the emporium just before closing time, found an opportunity of secreting himself, obtained all the necessary keys from his friend, and cleared off with something over a hundred pounds as his reward.

'And what became of your friend?' I inquired.

'Never see 'im since. I unnerstand he got the push,' replied young Alf.

'And he did not get his share of the spoil?'

Young Alf's under jaw denoted impatience at the absurdity of the question.

'That little bit didn't last me long,' he continued, after a pause, during which I reflected on the unequal distribution of this world's blessings. 'I flew me kite pretty high for the first few days. Rigged meself out like the Duke of Barnet Fair, an' hired a slap up 'awse an' trap, an' drove up to Aldridge's in St Martin's Lane.'

Young Alf sat up in his chair, stuck out his feet, and made as though he were tickling up a high-stepper with a touch of the whip.

'Did me good to see the 'angers-on all tryin' to get the job of holdin' me 'awse's 'ead. I bought free animals at Aldridge's, 'cause I was always fond of 'awses. But I didn't know what to do wiv 'em, an' not long afterwards I sold 'em for next to nuffink, me bein' boozed at the time. So I didn't get much more out of that job than me pal – if that's any consolation to 'im.'

Young Alf nodded at the fire as one who casts regrets after wasted substance.

'But Jimmy fort I'd done the job about as neat as it could be done,' he continued more cheerfully, after a pause.

And then we fell to talking of Jimmy and his present prosperity. As I have told you, he is doing very well as a fence, and when he is finally gathered to his rest will be found a very warm man. The mention of Jimmy reminded me of a question which I had intended to ask young Alf. Jimmy, you may remember, carried a revolver in the days before increasing bulk rendered a more sedentary occupation than burglary advisable, and was quite prepared to empty it into the skull of anyone who stood between him and his swag. I wanted to know if young Alf had ever found it necessary to shoot.

In ordinary circumstances you might hesitate to ask a guest who is sitting with his feet on your fender if he has committed a murder. But a moment's reflection assured me that the circumstances were not quite ordinary, and that I might put the question, bluntly, without offence.

My conclusion was right. Young Alf saw nothing offensive, or even unusual, in my question, and answered frankly that whenever he had carried a revolver in the exercise of his profession, he had taken care that it should be unloaded.

'I'd do me stretch on me napper,' he said, 'but I don't want to do it wiv me neck. See?'

Young Alf enjoyed his joke amazingly, puffing out his cheeks and digging his hands yet deeper into his trouser pockets.

He then explained that it was only old hands who carried loaded revolvers and used them when in a tight place. A man such as Jimmy would certainly, if caught, get it served out to him pretty hot, being an old offender, well known to the police, and acquainted with many prison warders. Jimmy would rather swing than do a stretch of which he was not likely to see the end. But young Alf's case is different. He has youth on his side, and a clean sheet, so far as convictions for burglary are concerned. It would not pay him – at present – to throw his life into the scale against your money.

Besides, he has great faith in the efficacy of an unloaded revolver which is not compromised by the discovery of any cartridge whatsoever on the person. He holds that the mere look of the inside of a pistol barrel is enough to bring the average householder to his senses. This theory he enunciated as he crossed one leg over the other and accepted a second cigar. It is based on the assumption that the average householder, even though he sleep with a loaded revolver under his pillow, has not the pluck to pull the trigger on an emergency. This theory he had an opportunity of testing one night when he found himself unexpectedly in the bedroom of a householder who was a bit too sharp for him. Young Alf found himself covered with a revolver.

'Move, and you're a dead man,' said the householder, who was seated on the edge of his bed.

Young Alf was compelled to temporize.

'For Gawd's sake don't murder me, mister,' he pleaded. 'It's my first offence, an' you wouldn't send my soul to 'ell?'

The householder advanced slowly upon young Alf, giving him an excellent view of the inside of the pistol barrel. Young Alf determined to act on the assumption that the man was afraid to fire at him. He whipped out his own revolver.

'Now, guv'nor, it's your life or mine,' said young Alf. 'And it shan't be mine.'

In a moment the householder was down on his knees, begging young Alf to spare him for the sake of his little ones.

Young Alf consented to spare him, kept him covered while backing out of the door, and then scooted for all he was worth.

My own theory is that the householder's revolver was unloaded, and that he allowed himself to be bluffed. But in this young Alf does not agree with me.

'That didn't skeer me,' continued young Alf, "cause I was sure in me own mind that the bloke wouldn't let fly at me. Time I was skeered was one night at Glasgow – subbubs of Glasgow, it was. That was one of the curiousest fings ever I come across.'

I inquired how he came to be in Glasgow, and learned that he and Jimmy were travelling with a circus. Jimmy held that this was a very good way of looking round the country without attracting suspicion. Young Alf was employed in the stables, looking after the horses, an occupation which he found congenial. He quitted his employment rather abruptly, having ascertained that the proprietor of the circus, a man addicted to drinking very freely when the day's work was over, kept the treasury chest by his bedside. Young Alf waited for a night when his employer was more than usually drunk, gained access to his sleeping apartment through a skylight, and left Glasgow by the next train.

This, however, is by the way.

'It was when we was at Glasgow,' said young Alf, 'that it happened what I was goin' to tell you about. Jimmy'd kep' 'is eyes skinned for chances, an' one night 'e put me on to a job to work on me own. He'd got a 'ouse waxed in the subbubs, seein' it stood by itself, wiv a lawn all round an' French windys. Reg'lar burglar's frens, French windys, wiv no error. Didn't take me 'arf a mo to get inside; but soon as I was inside I fort I 'eard a step comin' down the stairs. So I got be'ind the curtains an' stood quiet. Course, you unnerstand it was quite dark. Well, the steps come down the stairs, an' the door opened, an' in come a young man in 'is night fings wiv a lamp. I stood quiet as I could, peepin' out 'tween the curtains, an' I see 'im put the lamp down on the table, an' go up to a box that was stannin' in the corner of the room close to where I was.'

Young Alf took his hands from his pockets and leaned forward, looking at me obliquely.

'He opened the box an' put 'is arms inside, an' I see 'im take out – what you fink I see 'im take out?'

'Gold – spade guineas?' I suggested.

'Bones.'

Young Alf shivered.

'Bones?' I exclaimed.

'Heap o' bones,' continued young Alf; 'sure as I'm settin' 'ere. Then 'e put 'em on the table, side o' the lamp, an' began settin' 'em one atop of the uvver, an' fittin' 'em togevver, careful like, an' after a bit there was a real skilliton stannin' up in the room. 'Ealfy, eh? Then the young man began playin' wiv 'is skilliton, like, pullin' out 'is arms, an' makin' 'im work 'is legs. That upset me, raver. On'y, course, I dursn't move from where I was. An' then 'e picked up the lamp an' went out again, leavin' me alone wiv the skilliton in the dark. Gawd's trewth, I nipped out quicker'n I come in, wiv no error.'

'But – did you ever find the explanation?' I asked.

'I told Jimmy 'bout it, an' Jimmy said from what 'e'd 'eard there was a lot of young doctors livin' in the house. It was a sort of lodgin'-'ouse, you unnerstand. An' Jimmy fort the young man'd been studyin' too 'ard, an' it'd got on 'is napper. See? Walkin' in his sleep, 'e was; that's what Jimmy finks. D'you fink so?'

I said the explanation seemed a reasonable one.

'But it made me feel – made me feel gashly,' said young Alf.

Even the memory was so gashly that young Alf consented to break through his rule and have a little whisky before he went, and under its influence he told me tales of gallantries that I would gladly set down if by any means they could be printed. As it is, you must take my word for it that young Alf has been loved by many, and has loved not a few.

It was nearly midnight when we parted. Young Alf glanced round the hall as I was letting him out, and asked if I kept that light burning all night.

I replied that I thought it was a sort of safeguard against burglars, and asked his opinion.

Young Alf said that for his part he would not be put off by finding a light in any house he had determined to work. In fact, he was always grateful to a householder who saved him the trouble of striking matches for himself. It is less nervous work when you can see what you are about. And on the whole he advised me to turn the light out.

We bade one another good-night, and young Alf went noiselessly down the steps.

'You know your way?' I asked.

Young Alf did not condescend to reply, but swung down the street, shoulders slightly hunched, his hands at his sides. From the opposite pavement a policeman watched him curiously.

I turned the light out.

18
The Constable Speaks

It was a very cold night; and I should not have gone out at all, but that my dog protested he was bored and wanted a change. So I put on an overcoat and went forth for his sake, and that is why I got into conversation with the policeman. For it must be admitted that my dog was not muzzled in exact accordance with the regulations, and the policeman, having remarked that it was a very cold night, remarked this as well.

He leaned genially over the gate, and said he was particularly interested in dogs, because he had one of his own; do everything but talk, that dog could; yes, he could smell him (for my dog was sniffing the official calves); curious things, dogs. Lucky dog, too, this one, not having a muzzle on, strictly speaking. And it was a bitter cold night, when you came on at ten and went off at six. Lonely, too. Well – thank you, it wouldn't come amiss. He looked this way and that way, and in no long time the door had closed behind the dog, the constable, and myself.

He nursed his helmet in the crook of his left arm, and said it was wonderful what a dislike dogs have to muzzles; he, personally, did not hold with the regulation at all, only he was allowed no voice in the matter. Yes, he would have some soda-water with it, but a very little, and rather less whisky. You were always sure of getting a drop of good stuff in a private house, and a constable must be careful to keep a clear head. Not like the stuff you get in publics, especially in the publics over that way.

The constable jerked his head towards the back window,

141

through which you might chuck stones in the direction of South London.

'You can't be sure you haven't got more in your drink than you reckoned,' said the constable.

'You mean it may be fiddled,' I said.

'Fiddled, I mean,' said the constable.

'Do you know Lambeth?' I asked.

'I was stationed there two years,' said the constable.

'Then I suppose you know something of the Hooligans?'

The constable implied that he knew all about them that was worth knowing.

'I wonder if you ever came across a young friend of mine who does something in that line,' I said.

The constable set down his glass.

'Begging your pardon, sir,' he said. 'Meaning the young feller I see going away from here the other night?'

'You know him?'

'I was intending to ask you if you knew the sort of young feller he is. I've known him since he was that high.'

The constable indicated a point at about the level of his waistbelt.

'There's a many of his sort about here,' continued the constable. 'But down Lambeth way they're – well – they're a treat. And that young feller was about the warmest I ever did come across. Sneak anything he could see, that boy would. Cheeky, too. My word!'

The constable nodded reflectively.

'I remember seeing him hanging round a fish shop one day, and so I says to him, "Be off now," making like as if I was going to cuff him. Catch him? Couldn't get near him. And then he looks back with his hands stuck in his pockets, and says, "None of your bleedin' interference, constable, 'cause I won't tolerate it." Those were his very words. Not four foot high, he warn't, at the time. Not that. Well, so long as you know the sort of young feller he is, there's no harm done.'

'I don't think he'll try to burgle me,' I said.

The constable thought he must be going. No; he would not take any more. A drop of something didn't do you any harm on a cold night, but you had to be careful, and you were always sure of a good drop of stuff in a private house. Not like what you got in publics. Ah, getting drink from publics was how more than one of his mates that he could mention had come to grief.

The constable put his helmet upon his head, and went down the steps into the night. I had one or two questions to put to young Alf at our next meeting.

19
All for Her

But at our next meeting I had no opportunity of putting the questions that had occurred to me. Nevertheless, the evening was full of interest; for young Alf was to engage in a glove contest at the little boxing place off the Walk, and I was invited to witness his triumph.

It was Saturday night, and eight o'clock, and life in the Walk was at its zenith. I was first at the rendezvous, and strolled slowly along watching the haggling and chaffering at the barrows, wondering at the bawling butchers, and delighting in the children who danced to the jangle of the piano-organ. Lambeth Walk, as I have already told you, will provide you with everything you can reasonably require in life. Even when you die you need not go farther afield for your requirements, for the undertaker flourishes in the Walk, and rival artists set forth the advantages you will gain by placing yourself unreservedly in their hands. A series of photographs showed me what I could expect for five pounds, and the additional respectability I could attain for an extra two pound ten. Ornaments for my tomb beckoned me; I was especially attracted by the white artificial flowers in glass cases, and hovered from one undertaker's window to another making the final selection of the glass case that should mark my final resting-place.

Poetry, too, you may have; elegies to celebrate your virtues and waft after you the regrets of your relatives. Possibly you might have a specially hand-made elegy if you liked to pay extra for it. Those in the window are machine-made, and there are half-a-dozen varieties from which you may choose. They are stamped in black letters

144

on white plaques fancifully wrought in the shape of a
shield, a heart, or the section of a funeral urn. I had some
difficulty in deciding, but I think this is the one that I
should like my household to hang up in their drawing-
room when I am no more –

> A Light has from our Household gone,
> A Voice we loved is still;
> A Place is vacant in our Home
> That never can be filled.

From the display in the window I inferred that this was
the most popular of the obituary verses. The rhymes
fascinated me. Besides, it would be rather piquant to
choose and pay for my own panegyric. I was absorbed in
the contemplation of these verses, and trying to make up
my mind to go in and ask the price, when I was recalled to
the hubbub and tumult of the Walk by a voice at my
elbow.

'Wotcher!'

Young Alf is no adept in the flourishes of courtesy. He
can say what he means, more particularly when he does
not mean well. But his forms of greeting and farewell lack
polish.

We went down the Walk together, talking with some
difficulty in the crowd that surged between the barrows
and the shops.

Young Alf was a little paler than usual, and more carefully shaved. He was, I think, excited. But nothing showed
excitement but his increased pallor and the gleam in his
eyes as he talked to me in hurried snatches over his
shoulder. And as we went I gathered up the thread of
circumstance that led to the coming fight.

It was a fight with the gloves. But there was a bit of
needle in it. It was all over Alice.

'Alice?' I inquired.

'You know. 'Er at the cawfy-'ouse.'

Yes; of course I remembered.

And then it came out.

Young Alf was really in love this time; had been in love for some months, without a waver or a doubt. He had been walking with Alice. But when a boy is really in love, and is not merely mucking about, he is always a little ashamed of himself. That, I presume, was the reason why young Alf had said nothing of Alice for some time.

But there was a rival in the case, – one Ginger, who sold newspapers on the other side of the water. Alice, I gathered, had shown a decided preference for young Alf; but Ginger had been pestering Alice with unwelcome attentions, and young Alf had sworn to mark him.

Decidedly the evening promised fun.

We passed from the glare and blare of the Walk into a dimly-lighted side street, under a railway-arch, and halted before a narrow doorway cut in a big pair of gates.

'Frippence, if you ain't got a ticket,' said a boy who stood just inside.

I paid threepence, and stepped into cobble-stones, darkness, and an odour of horse-cloths.

'Strite on,' said the boy at the gate, as young Alf slipped away from my sight.

The light guided me, and the hum of voices, and in a moment or two I was stumbling from the gloom into a sort of huge box, lighted by a couple of gas-jets suspended from the ceiling.

'Frippence extry 'cross there,' cried another boy. I paid the threepence, and found myself entitled to a seat on a carpeted bench at the corner of the ring, which is not a ring, but a square. I looked round, a little dazzled by the sudden glare of gas.

Three or four hundred faces, packed in tiers, which rose

from each side of the ring. In the lowest tier small boys, in
all varieties of undress, who stood and rested their chins on
the rope. Above them, row upon row of faces, mostly
young, and frequently dirty, with here and there the pink
shirt and pallid complexion of a flashily-dressed Jew, –
and not a woman's face among them.

The piece of the evening was not yet on; but we were
mildly interested in the curtain-raiser.

In the sawdust a couple of youngsters were sparring –
boys of thirteen or thereabouts – glorious in the small-
clothes of the ring, and enjoying themselves hugely. It
takes a smack in the face to make a Lambeth boy laugh,
and these infants laughed aloud as the gloves (strictly
regulation gloves, as we were assured) got home upon their
faces.

The genial proprietor stood, slightly swaying, in one
corner, giving words of encouragement.

'Garn, yer young devils,' he said, pleasantly. 'You can
get 'ome oftener'n that. When you see a place, you 'it it,
'ard; bleed'n' 'ard. That's the way.'

He nodded approval, and the boys with their chins on
the ropes wagged their heads, knowing that old Mugs has
stood up to Jem Mace in his time, and that the words that
fall from his lips are golden.

No millionaire in London was prouder that night than
those two small boys who had concentrated the eyes of
their world upon them. And the proudest moments were
when they retired on the call of time to their respective
corners, laid themselves back in their respective chairs,
and had a full-grown man to flap a towel in their faces.
Only one man, who walked from one to the other. For boys
of thirteen cannot expect more than half a second. But he
flapped the towel; and the little boys, as you could see, lay
back, opened their mouths, dropped their arms, and
thought of Jem Mace.

'Don't forget 'em, gentlemen,' cried the master of the ceremonies, when time was finally called.

Halfpennies into the sawdust, and two panting little boys picking them up.

'Say thank you kindly, gen'l'men all,' said the master of the ceremonies.

The little boys stood, still panting, in the middle of the ring. It is nervous work, that maiden speech; but they brought it off, squeakily and together, and retired into a corner where they were decently hidden from about a third of the audience to change their clothes. Here a couple of brawny young men were stripping to the waist; Bill Smith of Wapping and Tom Lodge of Limehouse – so the master of the ceremonies announced, as they stepped into the ring to give an exhibition of sparring, and I was not surprised to learn that they were sailors. They danced about the ring, ducking and feinting with the greatest good humour. And when Tom Lodge got Bill Smith's face under his arm, tapped it gently to give him a taste of what would happen if it were serious, and invited him to say his prayers we all laughed heartily.

The cap round for coppers, and the two sailor lads, who had scarcely stopped laughing all the time with the sheer joy of strength and skill, went back to their corner to resume their shirts and coats.

Already the corners were occupied by the next pair, Sammy of Stockwell, and young Spooney of Bermondsey. A six-round contest. As the lads crossed, shook hands, and set to work they looked well matched. Sixteen years old, or thereabouts, clean and neat, not an ounce of superfluous flesh on them. A boy learns something besides courage and agility in the boxing ring. He learns to wash himself. Every lad who stepped into the ring that evening looked as bright and fresh as a new pin. Little personal vanities, too, may be noted. Young Spooney, for instance, had decorated his black small-clothes with pink ribbons, and his immaculate white shoes were laced with pink.

But Sammy of Stockwell did not show good sport, and murmurs arose among the audience before the first round was half-way through.

'When's Sammy goin' to start?' sung out a voice.

Old Mugs, the proprietor, called for silence.

But the murmurs continued as Sammy backed round and round the ring.

"It 'im, Sammy, 'it 'im!' called his second.

And then old Mugs ducked under the ropes, laid a heavy hand on Sammy, pulled off his gloves, and pushed him out of the ring.

'Them that wants to spar *can* spar,' remarked old Mugs, 'but damme if a boy's goin' to spar 'ere an' call it fightin'.'

Old Mugs looked round for approval, and got it, full measure and running over.

Sammy had retired hurriedly to cover his shame and nakedness. And here was young Spooney standing disconsolate in the middle of the ring, gloved hands hanging unemployed at his sides. Was he to be done out of his fight? Must he exchange his tasty small-clothes with the pink ribbons for patched, prosaic trousers before the company had had time to note their magnificence?

'Lemme tike 'im on.'

We all turned in the direction of the voice, and saw a shirt dragged hastily over a head, a hitch to a pair of trousers, and a reef of a belt taken in.

Old Mugs nodded assent, and young Spooney, looking much relieved, retired to his corner, in order that the conventions might be observed.

The master of the ceremonies whispered an inquiry to the new-comer, and then announced 'Sparkey.'

'Of Lambeth,' added Sparkey.

'Sparkey of Lambeth, and young Spooney of Bermondsey. Time.'

And for the next five minutes there was not a dull instant. Sparkey was no match for young Spooney, and he knew it. He was certainly not more than fourteen; a chubby-faced boy, with a firm jaw and a good pair of eyes. But he was two years younger than young Spooney. and nearly two inches shorter. Nevertheless, a boy does not often get a chance like this, even if he sits and waits for it every Saturday evening in the year.

Sparkey was game enough, taking his banging like a man, and even getting home now and again on to young Spooney's face. But, on the whole, young Spooney had it his own way, and early in the third round knocked Sparkey senseless over the ropes, close to the corner at which I was sitting. Sparkey lay quiet for a bit. Then he opened his eyes. Someone pulled him on to his legs.

'I know'd I wasn't class enough for young Spooney,' he said, blinking his eyes.

'Never you mind, cocky, you done yer level,' said old Mugs. 'Now, gen'l'men, don't forget the loser.'

We made it up to Sparkey in coppers, young Spooney courteously collecting for his late opponent. And as Sparkey pulled on his shirt again in the corner, which was technically out of view, he looked as though he thought life was not such a bad thing after all.

''E'll be 'eard of, that boy will,' said a voice behind me.

A shrewd, unshaved face, with a pair of piercing eyes, met me as I turned.

'Sat there night after night lookin' for 'is chance. Ah, everything comes to them as waits.'

A shuffling of feet, and a general squeeze up as the very last dozen that the room would hold elbowed their way in. Expectation was at its height. The benches that rose in tiers to the ceiling were crammed with eager heads in

caps that leaned forward, and showed here and there
a surreptitious cigarette, in spite of the periodical
cry from old Mugs: 'No smokin', gen'l'men, if *you*
please!'

Aloft, close by the entrance, the calm cap and serene
face of an inspector. For, so far, we are well within the
limits of the law, and entitled, as British subjects, to
police protection. Below, the little boys craned their necks
over the rope, until old Mugs swayed round and swept
them back.

Suddenly, I was aware of young Alf by my side, in his
chair at his own corner. But young Alf translated. Young
Alf in pink breeches, white stockings and shoes. Young Alf
holding out his hands superciliously for his second, a
bullet-headed ruffian, to put his gloves on. Young Alf paler
than ever, but with eyes that whipped round the ring and
settled with a blaze of fury on Ginger in the other corner.
He neither spoke to me nor looked at me, but dropped his
gloved hands and waited.

The master of the ceremonies stepped forward, cleared
his throat, and braced his voice for an effort. The buzz of
comment dropped.

Was there any objection to our old friend Mat Mullins
as timekeeper?

None whatever. And Mat Mullins was entrusted with a
watch. Mat Mullins was a heavily-built man in a grey
muffler. The good-humoured lines of his face were strongly
marked out with coal-dust.

As to judge, there could be no objection to old Spooney,
if he didn't mind being called old Spooney, seeing that his
son—

Carried by acclamation. And old Spooney, who turned
out to be the shrewd-eyed man who sat behind me,
deprecated the compliment, and accepted the office.

'I don't shove meself forward,' said old Spooney, 'but if

there's no better man—' That settled it, for we drowned his apodosis in a shout.

Again the master of the ceremonies braced himself for an effort.

'I beg to interjuice to your notice,' he said, resting one hand on the ropes and fixing an eye on a corner of the ceiling, 'Paddy of Lambeth, and Ginger of – of—'

'Camb'well,' prompted Ginger, from his corner.

'And Ginger of Camb'well. A six-round contest, fought strictly under the Marcus o' Queensberry's rules. During this 'ere contest I must arst you to keep silence, gen'l'men all. 'Tween the rounds you can shout.'

We were all very silent now.

Mat Mullins, the timekeeper, leaned forward with the watch between two huge fists.

Old Mugs beamed pleasantly about him from the vacant corner under the entrance.

'I know you'll be 'ighly amused,' he said. 'They're good uns. Their fathers bred 'em awright.'

'Seconds out,' said Mat Mullins.

Old Mugs ducked under the rope.

'Time.'

Young Alf, known for the moment as Paddy, was up in an instant, crossed, touched the gloved hand of Ginger, and sprang at him with a tigerish gleam in his eyes.

It was no good calling for silence; for we all knew the boys meant business, and we stood up and shouted wildly. Young Alf was going for a knock-out for all he was worth, and Ginger nearly went down before his first onslaught. It was a wild and furious round. A whirl of fists, a grapple, a break away, a spring together, a frantic dance at the far corner of the ring, and – 'Time!'

'Put yer tongue right aht,' said young Alf's second, getting to work with the sponge, while young Alf lay back

152

in his chair, drawing deep breaths. Then flap-flap with the towel, and again—

'Seconds out!'

A final flap with the towel, for every breath of air is valuable.

'Time!'

Young Alf's second is under the rope, and the boys are at it again.

They are still as fresh as paint, and again young Alf goes for Ginger, like a demon chased by Furies. But Ginger – I must take a look at Ginger. He is a little taller than young Alf, but slighter; for young Alf, stripped for fighting, shows a torso in which all the muscles stand out as though carved in marble. A lad with dark hair, a calm face, and a somewhat sinister smile. Such was Ginger. And Ginger had more science than young Alf. Guarding his head from damage he brought out a rosy flush on the marble of young Alf's ribs. I wondered why they called him Ginger, and I put the question to old Spooney at the end of the second round.

''Cause 'e's a bit of a 'ot un, I eggspect,' said old Spooney.

It was not to be a walk over for young Alf. By the fourth round the boys came up panting, and we rose and shrieked encouragement and abuse as young Alf went again for Ginger's face, and Ginger put his work in upon young Alf's ribs. Ginger was smiling unpleasantly, and young Alf's cheeks were puffing, while his eyes gleamed luridly.

On a sudden the shouting gathered itself into a single volley of sound, – a roar of protest, – and young Alf thought better of it.

He was not fighting scientifically; he fights to win; but there are some rules you may not break.

Old Spooney's breath was on my cheek.

'Time!'

Young Alf's breath is coming thick and fast now, as he lies back in his chair, and permits the bullet-headed ruffian to mop his face, and squirt water upon it from his mouth. He turns his head, and catches encouragement from my eyes.

'I'll do it, if I bust me guts,' pants young Alf. 'Stick yer tongue aht, an' don't talk,' says his second. 'Blarst yer,' he adds, as he pursues his kindly office. And again the conscientious coal-heaver who holds the watch calls—

'Time!'

Again young Alf leaps upon Ginger. Hard pounding this time, though Ginger is still smiling ominously. Hard shouting, too, for we are getting near the end. But suddenly someone shouts louder than the rest. It is old Spooney behind me. Some one also leaps into the ring, and pulls young Alf off Ginger, whom he has driven into a corner.

'Glove slipped.'

It is tied up. Young Alf looks furtively round him during the operation, and I wonder if it was an accident.

At it again, both trying to drive the final blow home.

Old Spooney leans down to my ear.

'I never see a comicker, bleed'ner fight in all me life,' he says.

'Time!'

Young Alf is very pale, and struggling for breath. His second fills his mouth with water and sends it as from a fire hose into young Alf's face. Flap-flap with the towel, and at the word young Alf can just rise to his task. Ginger has to be propelled into the ring by friendly hands.

In less than half-a-minute Ginger slips, – he is down. We rise in our seats, and howl. But young Alf is too pumped to reach him before he has staggered to his feet again. The boys have fought themselves out; and when time is called, young Alf is feebly patting Ginger on the left ear, while Ginger is gently tickling young Alf in the ribs.

Another victory of science. For the verdict is with Ginger.

'Don't forget the loser, gen'l'men,' said the master of the ceremonies. And young Alf recovered sufficiently to carry round his cap for pennies.

'It won't end there,' said old Spooney, presently. 'They'll 'ave that out with the raws, sure's I'm talkin'.' I looked round for young Alf. He had disappeared, Ginger, too, was not to be seen. Already the corners were occupied by another couple of combatants; and a certain listlessness was noticeable in the audience. The great event of the evening was over.

I made my way with some difficulty to the exit. The police-inspector nodded to me as I passed.

'Good 'ealthy exercise, sir,' he said. Outside, four or five constables stood, beating their hands together; for it was a cold evening.

Beyond, the street stretched into gloom and emptiness. But under the gas-lamp at the turn stood a girl. I paused for a moment, uncertain of my course.

'Are you looking for Alf?' said the girl. I recognized the voice instantly. It was the voice I had heard at the end of Irish Court. 'I sin you with him lots of times,' she added, in explanation.

'You must be Alice,' I said. 'Where is Alf?'

'In there,' she replied, pointing with her finger. 'I can't go an' look at it. You go. Say I'm 'ere.'

A couple of lanterns gave light enough to show me a stable-yard. A dozen or so of partisans formed a ring. This time there was no noise, no seconds, no towel-flapping. Also there were no rules. They were fighting in savage silence. We, too, stood round tense and earnest, making no sound; for now at last we were breaking the law and disturbing the Queen's peace. It seemed to me a long time that I stood there watching the flicker of the lanterns on those two struggling figures. But probably only a minute or so passed before young Alf brought off his favourite manoeuvre in the kind of fighting where nothing is barred. With a quick butt of the head, and a raised elbow, he caught Ginger under the chin, and bore him to the ground, falling on top of him.

Young Alf rose and passed his arm across his lips. Ginger remained where he was.

That is an effective stroke, if you have cobbles underneath on which to crack your adversary's skull.

Someone brought a pail of water and threw it over Ginger, who presently sat up and looked about him.

Outside, under the lamp-post, I found Alice adjusting young Alf's neckerchief.

'You won't 'ear no more from Ginger, not for a bit,' said young Alf. 'Now then, come on; don't 'ang about.'

They walked away together. Alice looked proud, – and so happy!

20

Outrunning the Constable

We were sitting in the pleasant room, and young Alf was
discoursing of policemen and their ways, for which he has
small respect.

Stimulated by questions I had asked, he told me with
great relish of a certain little trick he has frequently
played, which no constable has ever been able to get over.

A constable may not drink on duty. But most constables
want a drink at about closing time, and reckon on getting
it, and getting it without payment. It is etiquette for the
policeman to tender a coin, whether he wants beer or a
'bus-ride. But 'bus-conductor and bar-man alike wave
aside the proffered copper. Doubtless they have their
reward. Young Alf tells of a constable who always uses the
same penny for his nocturnal beer. That penny, he says,
must already have purchased a dray load of four ale, and
it will probably retain its purchasing power undiminished
until the constable claims his pension.

With these facts young Alf plays.

You take the constable's penny – for of course he does
not make personal application at the bar – and, instead of
returning with the beer, you slope out by another door.
Thus you gain a penny, and have the laugh of the constable, who dare not make a fuss about it. That is the simplest way of working the trick. You may complicate it by
scoring off both cop and publican. You enter the house,
and, tendering a penny, ask for the policeman's beer to
take outside; selecting a moment when there is no policeman outside. You return the penny to your pocket, take
the beer outside, and drink it. Then you bring back the

tankard, and depart in peace – to the next public-house, if you are still thirsty. By this means you get your drink for nothing, and have the additional joy of knowing that the copper will probably miss his beer that night.

Oh no; cops are no account. Such was the substance of young Alf's judgement. What would you expect when, so soon as a cop joins the force, he is put on to a particular division where his dial is soon as familiar as the clock-face at Westminster? Why don't they shift a Lambeth cop to Stratford, and give a Drury Lane cop a turn in Lisson Grove?

Young Alf grew quite furious at the folly of those who should pinch him, and neglect their duty.

Splits, too! what is the use of a split in uniform trousers and the regulation seven-league boots? Why, there isn't a split in South London, that hasn't had his image gone through before he has been at the job a day. Even if he rigs himself out as a Salvation Army captain. Just as well known as the podgy old wobblers who walk their beats to kill time while their pensions ripen.

Didn't I ever hear how he clean picked the split that wanted him to peach? No? Well, I must hear that.

'There was a ole split that used to hang abart the gallery at the Canterbury,' said young Alf, 'an' he was always ars-tin' me wevver I couldn't sell 'im somefink. An' now an' then I'd give 'im a little bit that I could do wivout for a bob. See? Well, me an' four uvver boys 'd got raver a big job on down Dulwich way, an' we wanted the splits put off it. 'Cause I was sure in me mind that they'd been smellin' around. So I took on the job of keepin' the coast clear, finkin' I could ring in me tale awright. An' jest as I fort, the split was hangin' abart outside the gallery at the Canterbury.

'Soon as he sees me, he says, "Good evenin', me lad.

Goin' to 'ave somefink wiv me?" he says. "Thanks," I
says. "I don't mind if I 'ave a cocoa."

'An' wiv that I walks up to a stall 'andy.

' "Got anyfink nice you can sell me tonight?" he arsts,
while I was drinking me cocoa.

' "Not for tonight," I replies.

' "When?" he says.

' "I fink I know of somefink for temorrer," I says.

' "Fink?" he says, suspicious.

' "Well, is it good enough?" I arsts.

'Long an' short of it was, I told 'im just the time we'd
got our job down for, on'y tellin' 'im a place on Clapham
Common, 'stead of Dulwich. See? I couldn't pull his ear
down for more'n a bob on'y he promised me somefink good
if it come off awright. End of it was that 'im an' four or five
more splits met me jest at the right time down Clapham
Common. 'Arf-past eight, it was. An' it wasn't till close on
ten that they began to show they fort they'd been made a
mark of. Goin' strong on the wrong scent they was, wiv
no error. Be that time our lads 'd done their little job
proper. Course, I didn't get nuffink furver for me infamation, an' I expect the splits fort a lot, eh? On'y there
wasn't no evidence. See? Case of clean pick; don't you
fink so?'

Thereupon young Alf waxed contemptuous of the ways
of splits.

'Oh, they ain't no use 'gainst a smart boy,' he continued,
rolling his shoulders from side to side in scorn. 'Why, when
I wasn't more'n fifteen, there was a split come up to me,
fren'ly like, an' arst me if I wouldn't 'ave a drink 'longer
'im. I said I didn't know 'im, but I didn't mind. Know
'im! I knowed 'im awright. Smell 'im 'arf-way up the
street.

' "Well," 'e says, "you like to do a little job for me?"

' "What as?" I arsts, tumblin' at once, you unnerstand.

' "Well," 'e goes on, "I've 'eard you're a clever little hook—'

' "Look 'ere, you stow that," I says. "Take me for a thief, do you, 'stead of a 'ard-workin' young man? Lemme tell yer I've more'n 'arf a mind to give you in chawge for inciting me to commit a felony." Making out as if I was angry. See? An' wiv that 'e never said annuver word an' slunk out of the 'ouse. Finkin' 'e'd catch me like that! See, I knowed somefink of the ways of the law, even if I wasn't more'n firteen.'

'But it ain't all lavender goin' on beat round the Walk,' continued young Alf, when he had refreshed himself with ginger-beer. 'I shan't forget the time when we was 'aving a bit of a game near the bottom of a alley that turns out of the Walk. There was eight or nine of us, an' finkin' about the cards, we didn't spot the cop 'fore 'e was right on to us. Raver a slippy cop, 'e was, in his way. He was jest making a pounce at the cards we was playing wiv when one of the boys sings out 'Dust-bin'! There was a big dust-bin in the corner, wiv a cover over it that fastened wiv a kind of catch. In less than 'arf a mo, we 'ad the copper up-ended an' pitched into the rubbish 'ole, and shut the lid down. We filled 'is 'elmet wiv any muck we could find, an' set it atop, like they put a soldier's 'elmet on 'is cawfin. We didn't put 'is truncheon wiv it, 'cause one of the boys ran that into a sort of curiosity shop for a tanner. Then we fort 'e might be firsty in the dust-'ole, so we kep' 'im supplied wiv water. Free or four buckets full we poured in. From what I unnerstand, he put in the best part of an hour of duty-time in the dust-bin; an' then an inspector missed 'im off the beat, an' ran on to 'is 'elmet an' let 'im loose. 'Ealfy, wasn't it?'

This did not betoken any special dislike of the policeman who was immured in the dust-bin, as young Alf subsequently explained to me. It was only part of the game, as tackling is part of the game of football. Indeed, young Alf reserves his animosity for the split, who does not nail his colours to the mast, but acts in an underhand, secretive manner, pretending, on occasion, to be an inoffensive plasterer having no connection with the mechanism of punishment. The policeman does not sail under false colours. He plays the game, and is entitled to be treated accordingly. You may sneak his beer; you may put him in a dust-bin, if you can catch him unawares and outnumber him to the point of safety; you may pour water upon him from buckets; you may subject him to discomfort and ridicule, as he will subject you to confinement and skilly if he can. But you should not kill him, so long as he plays the game; and the game has not lives for stakes. Such, I gather, are the views of young Alf and his associates. And statistics, as young Alf assures me, show that, in his time at least, no copper has been done to death by violence in Lambeth.

The police force has its notions of fair play, too. This you may learn from young Alf's experience. It is pleasant to hear young Alf paying a generous tribute of appreciation to the heart, if not to the head, of the police. He has waged incessant warfare against them. But the battle has been fought fairly and squarely, at least on the part of the constable, and young Alf is quite ready to admit that if he is caught he deserves his capture.

More particularly, the inspectors are always ready to give you a fair start and a fair run for your money.

With young Alf the illustration follows pat upon the statement.

There was that time when he was pinched for doing a bit of bashing. Disorderly, they called it, and drunk. He was quite in the wrong, he admits. For he ought not to have been drunk. Having regained his senses, he resigned himself to his fate; for he had no money wherewith to buy freedom, and foresaw the necessity of working out his salvation. His luck seemed to have deserted him, he reflected, as he watched a line of men drawn up, of which he himself was the extremity. A woman came in to identify a prisoner.

Young Alf, standing nearest to the door, spotted a detective near her elbow. And as the woman entered, he heard the detective say to her:

'Fourth from the end.'

Young Alf's sense of justice was stirred.

Before the woman had time to reach the fourth from the end young Alf had stopped the proceedings.

'Look 'ere, guv'nor,' he said to the inspector, 'I'm in 'ere meself for fightin', an' I want to see fair play.'

Then he told the inspector what he had heard. Thereupon the inspector ordered the woman out, and shuffled his pack of malefactors. One changed scarves with another, and young Alf clad himself in the coat of the fourth from the end and took his stand beside him.

Re-admitted, the woman failed to recognize any one, and the fourth from the end, having recovered his coat, went to his own place.

In due course young Alf came before the beak, and, as he had anticipated, it was forty shillings or a month. For young Alf is an expert in the arithmetic of crime, and knows quite well how far he may go for forty shillings, and what will cost him a stretch. But young Alf had not forty farthings upon his person. This would not have mattered if it had been Lambeth, or Southwark, or perhaps even Wandsworth. For the lads would have been there to limber up. Unfortunately, young Alf was in a district where he was, so far as he knew, friendless. He felt it must be a month.

And then the extraordinary thing happened.

A woman stepped forward and paid the fine. A woman who was quite unknown to young Alf. Outside the court he met her.

Young Alf is not an adept in the language of courtesy and compliment, and from his own account of the incident I gather that he simply stared at her.

'That was my old man you got off,' said the woman. Then she kissed him.

I got that out of young Alf with some difficulty; but she kissed him.

So virtue found its reward. So, too, is the character of the policeman vindicated. He plays fair.

But though the cop's heart is in the right place, his head is weak. You can kid him – oh! you can kid him, straight. Any boy of ordinary smartness can kid a copper, provided that he has not got the swag upon him at the time. What price the fake he worked when the slop came on him suddenly while the lads were at work on the roof? Eh?

What was the fake?

Young Alf leaned forward and told me, with many cunning side glances.

'One night some of the lads was workin' on a job on some flats up Bloomsbury where there was repairs goin' on. I was down in the street below, keepin' a eye, an' I fort they wasn't workin' so quiet as they oughter 'ave. An' jest as I stopped to listen, a cop come up be'ind me wiv 'is silent shoes.

' "D'you 'ear anyfink up there?" 'e says, givin' his 'elmet a nod towards where the lads was workin'.

' "I fort I did," I says. "I was jest listenin'.'

' "I want you," he remarked, "to go up wiv me to the top of this yer buildin'; I've got my suspicions that there's somefink wrong."

163

' "Well," I says, "that's a job I don't care about, guv'nor. I don't want to 'ave a 'ole bored froo me wiv a six-shooter. Wouldn't be 'ealfy for me."

'Course I wanted to make 'im skeered. See?

' "I don't much relish it meself," 'e says. "But if I arst you in the Queen's name, you got to come. An' if we make a capture, it'll be worf your while."

'I see be his manner 'e was skeered. So I made out as though I was gettin' up me pluck, an' then I says to him—

' "Well," I says, "I'm a bit used to roofin' be trade. You gimme your lantern, an' I'll nip up an' crawl round an' see what's goin' on."

'He was more'n willing. Handed over 'is lantern, an' went an' hid 'isself round the corner where 'e couldn't see nuffink. Wiv that I nips up one of the ladders that was stannin' 'gainst the flats, an' give the lads the wheeze. Told 'em to grease off be anuvver ladder at the back soon as I'd rung in me tale to the cop down below. See? Then I worked me way back to where the cop was hidin', an' rang in me tale 'ow they was layin' be'ind a chimbly an' we could catch 'em if we went sawft an' made a spring.

'Didn't 'arf fancy the job, the cop didn't. But 'e come up awright, me carryin' the lantern in front. An' there we was, crawlin' round the roof like a bloomin' pair of cats. An', when we come to the chimbly, there wasn't nobody there.

' "Well," I says, "I fort I see somebody layin' be'ind there; but I s'pose it was on'y me fancy."

'So down we come again, an' I cracked on to the copper about 'is pluck goin' on to the roof like that, an' 'e thanked me for me 'elp an' sprung a bob for me trouble. Oh, you can kid a cop soon as look at 'im. Don't you make no meestike.'

Young Alf leaned back in his chair, stuck his hands into his trouser pockets, and spat straight into the middle of

the fire to show his contempt for the head – not the heart –
of the police. I inquired whether this was one of the cam-
paigns organized by Jimmy.

Young Alf replied that Jimmy had nothing to do with
that adventure.

'Where is Jimmy living now?' I asked.

Young Alf's under jaw protruded ominously. You know
that Jimmy is thriving as a fence. But young Alf did not
give me his address. I learned, however, that Jimmy,
becoming more cautious with increasing years and bulk,
objected to personal dealings with his clients. Jimmy
recognizes the admirable organization of the Parcel Post.
If you get a bit of stuff – say at Surbiton, – you do not
bring it to town in a cart, or by any such crude and open
method. You pack it up, affix the requisite number of
stamps, and all the Queen's horses and all the Queen's men
will combine to convey it safe and sound to Jimmy. That
is, if you know what address to put on your parcel. This is
an essential if you wish to deal with Jimmy. For Jimmy is
a fanatic about the Parcel Post. He maintains that there is
no safer and surer service in the world.

The Course of True Love

It was advisable that Alice should be married to young Alf forthwith. But there were difficulties in the way. Alice's father did not approve of the match even in the special circumstances, and threatened bashing. And Alice's father, if I may credit young Alf's rapid sketch, is not a man to be trifled with. He is a book-maker of unbridled temper, and is accustomed to be master in his own house. Towards nightfall, when Alice's mother can still argue but can no longer stand, his remedy is ingenious and effective. He slings a rope – so young Alf tells me – round her chib, and fastens it to a hook in the wall. Then Alice's mother can stand, but can no longer argue. A man, I gather, of strong character, but not lovable. A husband and father to inspire fear rather than affection.

The opposition of the book-maker was a serious difficulty, but, with the combined forces of Alice and her mother, not an insuperable one. Alice was very anxious for the wedding: Alice's mother, so long as she could stand, was insistent. Young Alf didn't care either way.

So the banns were put up without the knowledge of the book-maker with the unbridled temper, and young Alf was devising a scheme for sneaking the book-maker's pony and cart in order that the ceremony might be carried out with a bit of class.

Meanwhile I was bidden to inspect the nest which young Alf was feathering for his bride.

It wanted but a few days to Christmas when we met at about eight o'clock outside Vauxhall Station, and it was then that young Alf told me of the difficulties which lay in his path to matrimony. The opposition of the book-maker did not trouble him much. The problem of furniture was much more important, and young Alf did not find it at all easy to pick up the precise things that Alice wanted, at the exact price he was willing to give.

'I want one of them brooms,' he remarked, nodding his head at a shop, the doorway of which was barred by the form of the proprietor. 'An' I 'aven't 'ad a chance to sneak one yet.'

He was troubled, too, at the necessity of purchasing a bed. With all his ingenuity he failed to see how he could acquire one in the ordinary way. So he had taken one on the hire system, paying a small sum down and engaging to pay instalments of five shillings a month.

'It's awright s'long as you pay *somefink*,' was his consoling reflection.

We turned twice, young Alf keeping slightly in front, according to his custom.

'I fink a lot of my gal,' he said, glancing back over his shoulder.

I replied that I had no doubt she deserved the best he could say of her.

'She deserves a better chap than what I am,' he said.

'Knows 'ow to 'old 'er tongue,' he continued, presently. 'I never told you 'ow she 'eld 'er tongue, did I?'

I said I had not heard the incident.

'Look 'ere, I'll tell yer,' he said. 'You know Ginger, – 'im what I fought the uvver night?'

'That was about Alice, wasn't it?'

'Nor it wasn't the first time there's bin a bit of a row over Ginger. I don't fink Alice liked Ginger; least, not like she liked me. But 'e was always messin' about after 'er. See? Well, one mornin' I got infamation that Alice'd gone to the Canterbury wiv Ginger the night before. I dessay there wasn't no 'arm in it, an' I ain't so sure in me own mind that she went wiv 'im at all. On'y that was 'nough for me. An', meetin' 'er next evenin' down China Walk, I arsts 'er what the 'ell she meant by walkin' wiv Ginger 'stead o' me. See? An' then I jest gives 'er two for 'erself; one in each eye. See? Well, Alice, she run off 'ome, an' got into bed quick as she could, an' made out as if she was asleep. 'Cause I'd marked 'er, you unnerstand. Presently, in comes 'er muvver, bein' a bit barmy, an' finds Alice layin' in bed makin' out as if she was asleep. So 'er muvver says – "Git up, you lazy 'ussy," she says, "layin' there like as if you was a lidy," she says.

'Alice says she wouldn't, an' put 'er face unnerneaf the cloves. An' wiv that, 'er muvver took an' fetched 'er a clip over the 'ead. See?

'Well, next mornin', Alice's eyes was stannin' out proper wiv the smack I'd give 'er. An' soon as 'er muvver see 'er, she fort of 'ow she'd landed Alice the night 'fore, an' nuffink'd do for 'er but she must mess Alice about, an' kiss 'er, an' 'ug 'er, an' say:

' "Oh, my darlin', to fink I should 'a' marked yer like that!"

"Course she was sober then, an' when she's sober Alice's muvver's as kind-hearted as you please.'

'And all the time it was you who had – marked her?' I said.

Young Alf stopped short.

"Course it was,' he said. 'That's what I mean; an' – look 'ere.'

We had halted under a lamp-post, and young Alf's eyes were gleaming in this light.

'Alice never said nuffink about it. What you fink o' that?'

I groped in vain for the appropriate answer, while young Alf's eyes were fixed on my face.

'I fort a lot o' that,' he said, magnanimously, and turned to resume the walk.

As we went along he confided to me something of his plans for the future, when he should have settled down in his own kip with a wife and such sticks as he could collect.

He had by some means acquired a pony and a barrow, and with these he would make his way in the world. With a barrow and a pony a boy may do a lot. He has a stake in the country, and is no longer as the proletariat.

By what means had he acquired the pony and barrow? The question elicited no reply; and I feared the worst. He would go in for selling green-stuff.

'Then do you mean to go straight now?' I asked.

'I dessay I shall sneak a bit now an' then,' replied young Alf. 'Stan's to reason. See, there's lots o' boys makes a good livin' gettin' on to the tail o' market wagons, an' rollin' off wiv somefink they can sell wivout a loss. Peas a tanner a peck! See?'

He contemplated but half a reformation, at most. He would sell green-stuff, which is a sufficiently honest employment. But he did not intend to buy it first.

'We're close there,' said young Alf, placing a hand on my arm. 'When you come in, don't you arst me where I got the fings. You swank as I 'ad 'em give me. See?'

'But,' I said, 'doesn't Alice – I mean, does Alice think—'

'It's awright if she doesn't know,' he replied, rather impatiently. 'An' she never arsts no questions. Knows 'ow to 'old 'er tongue, Alice does. On'y if she knows I've got anyfink on the crooked – like a bit of jool'ry I give 'er, – she doesn't seem to take no interest in it. See?'

He stopped by a ground-floor window, put his ear to it for a moment, and tapped.

'Awright,' he said.

He drew me back a step or two, to where a door fronted

immediately upon the street. We waited. In a few moments it was opened by Alice.

'What ho!' said young Alf.

'I was listenin', ' said Alice.

Where did that girl get her voice of liquid gold?

We entered, and Alice resumed her seat, drawing her shawl round her. A single candle, already nearly at its last flicker, lightened her vigil. The room contained three chairs, a table, a few odd pieces of crockery, a strip of carpet, and the bedstead of which young Alf had spoken. But Alice directed my attention to the mantelpiece.

'I've jest been puttin' 'em up,' she said. 'Seems to brighten up the place – makes it more 'ome-like, don't it?'

Young Alf walked over to the mantelpiece.

'Can't 'ardly see 'em,' he said. 'Let's 'ave annuver candle.'

'Got a penny?' said Alice.

Young Alf hunted in his pockets and drew blank.

But the lack was supplied, and Alice went out in search of another candle.

Young Alf picked up the guttering light from the table, and held it aloft so that I might see and admire the pictures.

Nailed to the middle of the wall over the mantelpiece was a framed engraving of a pigeon, which young Alf had certainly not acquired by honest purchase. But there was a sentimental interest about it. For he had started the serious business of life, as you may remember, by sneaking pigeons. Beneath this, the photograph of a horse.

'That's a 'awse I got at Brighton,' said young Alf, holding the candle with one hand and with the other turning the light on to the picture. 'Sold it up 'ere in Lambef. It's workin' 'ere now.'

A photograph of young Alf and Alice, arm-in-arm, in very low tone, taken in Epping Forest. Another photograph of the book-maker with the unbridled temper. No. Certainly not a lovable man. A man to keep at a respectful distance. This piece of decoration was clearly Alice's idea, and young Alf swept the candle past it. To right and left of the book-maker a pair of coloured prints representing Christ Blessing the Loaves and Fishes, and Christ on the Sea of Galilee.

Alice returned; and the illumination was increased by a candle.

'Alf bought them,' said Alice, indicating the representations of Our Lord; ''cause I liked 'em.'

'Give a penny each for 'em,' said young Alf, in apology for being reduced to purchase.

Alice had resumed her seat by the table, and sat with her shawl drawn closely round her. In the clearer light of the extra candle, I had my first view of her face.

Fair hair, dressed low over the forehead and the ears, after the fashion in vogue among the girls engaged in the manufacture of aerated waters; soft grey eyes – long recovered from the imprint of young Alf's fist; a mouth somewhat too large for absolute beauty, but well shaped; a figure which in a few months will be slim again. Altogether the sort of girl you may find by the hundred whereever there are streets and tramcars and factories. But her voice marked her off.

I wanted to hear it again; but my stock of small talk was unready. I could converse readily enough with young Alf; but when confronted with Alice, I realized that in all that related to the minor interests of life we were very far apart.

She sat quietly by the table, her hands in her lap, looking straight before her. Young Alf busied himself by shifting the respective positions of the pigeon and the horse over the mantelpiece.

'It's awright, isn't it?' said young Alf.

I said that it seemed very comfortable. To Alice I added that I wished her much happiness, and that I thought I must be going.

Alice rose, and we shook hands.

'Did I hear you was comin' – Monday?' she said. 'Alf'd be glad.'

Monday was Boxing day, – the day fixed for the wedding.

'And I'd be glad, too,' added Alice.

I promised my presence, and ascertained the place and hour of the ceremony.

Young Alf accompanied me to the door, as Alice returned to her chair. As we stood in the doorway he explained that the unbridled book-maker was due at some race-meeting or other on Boxing day; consequently, the pony and cart could be abstracted without difficulty, and the wedding ceremony carried out without the infliction of the threatened bashing.

'Half-past nine, then,' I said. 'I shall be there punctually.'

Young Alf looked back, and pulled the door behind him.

'What you fink if I didn't turn up?' he asked, with an oblique glance.

'I think you wouldn't get the little present I'm going to give you – when you're married,' I replied.

He said nothing for a few moments. I watched his eyes, as they glanced quickly this way and that way up and down the street.

'Once before,' he said, 'I've bin as far as the church door wiv a gal – and come away.'

22

Holy Matrimony

A dishevelled London. A London that had gone late to bed, and was yet scarcely fit to be seen. A London that blinked at me with eyes but half open. Such was the London that faced me as I waited for the omnibus that should convey me to Westminster, whence another would pass me on to the turning which led to the church whither I was bound. For it was the morning of Boxing day. Christmas day was over; so much you could see by the orange peel; and Boxing day was not yet really begun.

A strong wind was blowing; not a cold wind, but a wind that sought out every stray piece of paper, and made it caper and dance and twirl. The street was empty but for myself; the shops were shuttered; and it was altogether rather depressing, until the omnibus lumbered up, and the driver slowing down, from mere force of habit, lashed the window with his whip. At present, I was the only passenger. The conductor clambered on to the roof to take my fare. When he had given me my ticket, he stood for a few moments contemplating the back of the driver.

'Bangkoldy, Bill, Bangkoldy! Well, it fair knocks me,' he said, jerking his head backwards, with the air of one who finds fortune fall below his hopes.

'Bit off, eh?' said the driver, looking over his shoulder.

We were not a cheerful party. We had some difficulty, too, in keeping our hats on.

'Blows like rain,' I remarked.

The conductor was swinging himself down again, but he halted on his way, and put a red face over the rail – a face designed for cheerfulness, but depressed by circumstances.

173

'Seems to me,' he said, 'the majority of people I've sin this mornin' wouldn't be much worse for a dash of cold water.'

'I'm just going to see a friend married,' I said; 'I hope the rain will hold off. Happy is the bride, you know—'

'Ah, your friend isn't the only one. Takes a bit of doin' to keep off being married Boxing day. Talking of merriage—' The conductor leaned one arm on the rail, and kept one eye on the pavement for possible passengers. He did not squint; yet he gave me the impression of looking in two directions at once. 'Talking of merriage,' he said, 'I heard rather a rich bit the other night. There was a bit of a knock-up down there at the 'Coach an' 'Awses', and a chap there was doing his turn, talkin' and arstin' riddles; you know what I mean. Singing, you know, only puttin' a bit in on his own 'tween the verses. Follow me? "What's matterimony after all?" he says. "Matter o' money." See what he meant? I expect it is with these upper circles, eh? But I ain't got no cause to complain. Lived in 'armony five years come Easter Monday, and that's more 'n most chaps can say. Well, 'ealth and 'appiness to your friend, – on'y, it's a bit too early, eh?'

He descended, looking a little more cheerful – cheerful enough to lean over and chaff the driver of a rival 'bus, which, being so far empty, was trying to pass him, and gather up any passenger that might be waiting at South Kensington Station.

'What are *you* doin'?' he said. 'Got a race 'awse?'

The driver of the opposition 'bus made a retort which did not reach my ears. It was inadequate; for our conductor became even more cheerful, and, when a girl in a waterproof clambered on to the roof, he came up, jammed his bowler closer over his ears, in defiance of an extra gust of wind and said:

"Ail, smiling morn!'

Holy Matrimony

At Westminster Bridge, London was livelier. The south-wester was blowing down the river, playing the deuce with skirts, and making toppers a misery. What was to happen to the unlucky young man whose silk hat had been blown into the river? The 'bus rolls on, and I leave him to face his fate. But there are no shops open, and he has, I know, depended on that topper. What will She say? And what will he do? I am carried beyond the answer, and am borne into South London.

South London is well awake, and I am aware of genteel couples on the look-out for trams; of plodding family parties, mother with baby on her left arm; children, too, come upon the kerb, and wonder at the people who are bound for distant lands, such as Hampstead or the Zoo. Bicyclists too, by this time, male and female, recking nothing of the tram lines or the wind, and intent only on enjoyment. And what is this brougham with the flowers in the lamp? This, and another? We are in the wedding area; and we shout encouragement to them as they pass.

I swing myself off the 'bus, and make my way to the appointed church. A church in a wind-swept square, with a gravel path leading up to it, and hemmed in by iron palings. I walk up and down, waiting for young Alf. I am buffeted by the wind, and cannot light a pipe, but have no lack of amusement.

Couples walk up, flanked by humorous relatives; parties drive up, five in a hansom, brimming over the apron, a white ribbon tied in a tasty bow about the driver's whip. One couple come on bicycles, lean their machines against the wall by the porch, and enter, together with a gentle-manly-looking man who awaits them.

I watch them, and wonder if perchance young Alf is before his time and is already in the church. Into the dim church I peep, and there I see the surpliced clergyman tying human lives into knots, by the dozen at a time.

But young Alf and Alice were not among them. The wind strengthens, and the churchyard trees are bending to it and dropping their tribute of twigs. From the church the couples emerge, their relatives more humorous than ever, and their cabmen, flourishing their whips tied tasty with a white bow, say things that make you giggle and shake with laughter and say 'Now, then, cheese it.'

The hour hand of the clock is creeping towards ten, closing time. For even a South London clergyman has his limits.

The hour strikes. The last couple has walked away under the blessing of the Church; and the church is empty, but for a fussing verger.

And still no young Alf.

This is serious. Has young Alf refused to start? or has the unbridled book-maker got wind of the matter, sought out young Alf, and bashed him? or has he spent his wedding-fee in riotous living? It is scarcely likely that this would stand in young Alf's way.

But I must find out what has happened. I begin to walk uneasily in the direction of Vauxhall. At the first corner a clatter of hoofs comes down the wind, followed by a pony-cart, driven at full speed, and loaded to the tail-board. As it passes at a gallop, young Alf waves a whip at me; and, halting, I catch a flash of Alice's face from the back of the cart.

The party had gained the porch by the time I arrived again at the church. The verger was not at all sure that the vicar had not gone. Anyhow young Alf was very late. But he would go and see.

Alice, her mother, and the rest of them filed into the empty church, and sat down to wait the vicar's decision. Alice, resplendent in blue, with the loveliest feathers. Young Alf remained with me by the porch.

'Supposing you can't get married this morning?' I said.

Young Alf stooped down, picked up a stone, and threw it at a sparrow to show his indifference.

The difficulty had been with the pony-cart, it seemed. The unbridled book-maker had been somewhat overcome by the festivities of the season, had overslept himself, and started late for his race-meeting. His absence was the pivot of the marriage question, for young Alf could not put his hooks on the pony-cart until he had gone, and to be married without a bit of class would not do for young Alf.

'You give me away?' said young Alf, smoothing out his neckerchief – the blue with white spots – which had become disordered in the excitement of the drive.

'I can't very well do that,' I said, 'but I'll give Alice away with pleasure.'

Young Alf wanted a pin for his neckerchief; in a moment he had secured a drawing-pin from the notice-board, and a parish notice fluttered in the wind.

I could see the wedding-party sitting, silent and expectant, inside the church.

'What you fink o' this?' said young Alf, diving into his vest pocket and bringing it out – the ring.

It was thick, shiny, conclusive.

'Cost much?' I suggested.

'Likely,' said young Alf, 'got it Sat'dy night at a shop in the Walk. Got it easy.'

The verger came shuffling down to where the wedding-party waited. They rose and went forward.

'Come on,' I said.

Young Alf took a parting shot at a sparrow and we advanced together from the porch into the shadows of the aisle, up to the altar rails, where Alice stood expectant. The wind howled a bridal march.

The clergyman came wearily forward, hitching his surplice over his shoulders as he came, and we lined up;

Alice's mother, uncertain of her position, and tearful; young Alf, with shoulders slightly hunched, and holding his cap squeezed in his left hand; Alice with her hands dropped and clasped before her.

It was soon over. The clergyman crossed the Prayer-book with the ring – that ring! We knelt.Pious hands were waved in blessing over the kneeling pair; and Alfred Eric (the names gave me quite a start) and Alice Maud were pronounced man and wife in the name of the Father and of the Son and of the Holy Ghost. Amen.

The verger drove the wedding-party into the vestry. I dodged, and went without.

Outside, the wind was picking twigs from the church-yard trees, and sending them hopping down the path. It had been down all the side streets, gathering up waste paper and refuse of all kinds, which it sent careering round and round the church.

The minutes dragged heavily as I walked up and down, speculating upon the future of young Alf and his bride. I hoped he would be kind to her.

Ten minutes passed, and even the pony, standing in the road, was growing impatient, and snatching at the reins which were hitched to the churchyard railings.

I had been waiting nearly a quarter of an hour, when they came out by the vestry door.

"Ad a bit of a argyment wiv the parson,' said young Alf, in explanation. "Ow many shilluns was it 'e wanted, muvver?'

'I give you the money last night, last thing, if it was the last word I ever spoke,' said Alice's mother.

Young Alf gave me a quick glance and a wink.

'I told the parson I 'adn't got no shilluns,' he said, 'an' 'e let me off. Reckon 'e makes 'is little bit awright.'

Alice had climbed up behind again, her mother beside her. Young Alf and a male supporter mounted in front;

and indeterminate friends filled the vacant places. My wedding present was offered and accepted.

Young Alf cracked his whip, and, as the pony started with a willing effort, Alice handed her mother her pocket-handkerchief. I stood watching them as they pounded up the road. They swung round the square, and young Alf, looking back, waved his whip at me. And so young Alf turned the corner.

The End

OXFORD

MORE OXFORD PAPERBACKS

Details of a selection of other books follow. A complete list of Oxford Paperbacks, including The World's Classics, Twentieth-Century Classics, OPUS, Past Masters, Oxford Authors, Oxford Shakespeare, and Oxford Paperback Reference, is available in the UK from the General Publicity Department, Oxford University Press, Walton Street, Oxford, OX2 6DP.

In the USA, complete lists are available from the Paperbacks Marketing Manager, Oxford University Press, 200 Madison Avenue, New York, NY 10016.

THE PRIVATE MEMOIRS AND
CONFESSIONS OF A JUSTIFIED SINNER

James Hogg

Edited by John Carey

Written in 1824, James Hogg's masterpiece is a brilliant portrayal of the power of evil. Set in early eighteenth-century Scotland, the novel recounts the corruption of a boy of strict Calvinist parentage by a mysterious stranger under whose influence he commits a series of murders. The stranger assures the boy that no sin can affect the salvation of an elect person.

John Carey has edited the text of the novel from the unexpurgated first edition of 1824.

The World's Classics

MEMOIRS OF A WOMAN OF PLEASURE

John Cleland

Edited and introduced by Peter Sabor

Memoirs of a Woman of Pleasure (commonly known as Fanny Hill), is the most famous erotic novel in English. Since the original edition appeared in 1749, the proliferation of further editions, adaptations, and translations bears witness not only to the popularity of scandalous novels, but also the book's literary merit.

This is the first critical edition of the novel, and the first to present an accurate, wholly unexpurgated text. It includes an extensive bibliography and notes, and an introduction that illuminates the mysterious composition of the *Memoirs* and the life of its shadowy author.

The World's Classics

MEMOIRS OF A MIDGET

Walter de la Mare

Introduced by Angela Carter

'This book is an authentic masterpiece. Lucid, enigmatic, and violent with a terrible violence that leaves behind no physical trace . . . It may be read with a good deal of simple enjoyment and then it sticks like a splinter in the mind.' So writes novelist Angela Carter in her introduction to Walter de la Mare's elegiac study of the estrangement and isolation suffered by the diminutive Miss M.

Twentieth-Century Classics

ALSO IN OXFORD PAPERBACKS

ROMANTICS, REBELS AND
REACTIONARIES
English Literature and its Background
1760–1830

Marilyn Butler

This book takes a fresh look at one of the most fertile
periods in English literature, a half-century which produced
writers of the stature of Blake, Keats, Coleridge,
Wordsworth, Byron, Scott, and Jane Austen. Marilyn Butler
questions the validity of grouping such diverse talents and
personalities under the critical label 'Romantic', and instead
presents them to the reader both as individuals and as part of
a larger cultural landscape.

This is a highly original book which is sure to enlighten and
stimulate students of the period as well as the general reader.

An OPUS book